THE MORAL IMPERATIVES OF HUMAN RIGHTS

A World Survey

Edited by
Kenneth W. Thompson

UNIVERSITY
PRESS OF
AMERICA

Copyright © 1980 by Council on Religion and International Affairs

University Press of America, Inc.™

P.O. Box 19101, Washington, DC 20036

ISBN (Perfect): 0-8191-0921-5
ISBN   (Cloth): 0-8191-0920-7
LCN: 79-3736

INTRODUCTION

President Harry S. Truman spoke of the United Nations as the cornerstone of American foreign policy and President Jimmy Carter has described human rights as the moral foundation of his administration's foreign policy. Less than a quarter century after President Truman's affirmation, neither candidate in the presidential election of 1972 spoke out for the United Nations, and the American ambassador to the United Nations under President Ford saw in the General Assembly "the theater of the absurd." In Britain and in a few European countries political rhetoric on the United Nations fluctuated less wildly. Because the leaders of countries schooled for centuries in the statecraft of world politics claimed less for the New World institutions, they suffered less disillusionment.

Any final judgment of President Carter's human rights campaign would be premature, yet critics note a certain slackening in the invoking of universal principles and a tendency to apply them selectively as between friend and foe. The aim of the Human Rights Study Group of the Council on Religion and International Affairs has been the study of important and neglected dimensions of the problem, namely, the cultural and historical, the ethical and theological foundations of human rights in particular world regions. We have approached human rights in China and the Soviet Union, the Middle East and India, and Africa and Latin America in a spirit of inquiry. We have examined American policies of human rights historically, philosophically, and from the standpoint of American and Western constitutional theory, leaving to others policy proclamations or the prejudging of the success or failure of the Carter campaign. Our goal has been understanding, rather than the praise or blame that seemingly have been the motifs of many of the controversies surrounding the public and foreign policy debate.

Ideally, the kind of human rights inquiry advanced by the authors of the essays in this little volume should have preceded, not followed, the public debate. In the era of the founding of the American Republic, inquiries and discussions in constitutional and political theory antedated the Declaration of Independence and the Articles of Confederation and the creation of "a more perfect union." Not only were the founders conversant with the main issues in ancient and modern political theory, but they applied theory to practice with a sure sense of the relation of political ideas to practical realities. In some nations and for some civilizations the flowering of political theory has accompanied political experience broadening out, as legal philosophers proclaimed, from precedent to precedent. The golden age of American political thought, by comparison, was present at the founding, and it would be difficult to match the Federalist Papers with writings in the present era.

No serious observer would claim that a political and constitutional theory of human rights comparable to the wisdom of the founders could result from a modest study group initiated in the late 1970's by a little organization in the heart of Manhattan. What well-focused inquiries may provide, however, is the raw stuff of facts and information on vastly different political systems on which future human rights thought and policy might be based. In 1937 the President's Committee on Administration Management declared "the President needs help," and the work of the Brownlow Commission permeated every subsequent attempt at administrative reorganization. Whenever progress has been made in the reformulation of public policy, thought and discussion have preceded action.

The retreat from the stridency and half-considered actions of the administration's policy in the first months of its human rights campaign suggests that once again "the President needs help." For those who find themselves on the firing line, help may come in the form of the kind of policy reformulation undertaken by Secretary of State Cyrus Vance in his carefully drawn Georgia law speech. For those who are removed and detached from the satisfactions as well as the urgencies of immediate pressures in the political arena, help, if it can be accorded, must take a different form. If the outsider can help at all, his contribution must come in providing the factual basis for action.

The CRIA study group has called on a handful of the nation's respected authorities to examine the underlying context of human rights in the different cultures that make up the society of nations. The founders of the new American constitutional system were both nationalists and states rightists. They understood the needs and background of the nation as a whole as well as those of the separate states. *E pluribus unum* emerged from the recognition of both particularism and universalism.

Each national or regional authority presented his paper for criticism and discussion by theologians, cultural and political historians, and constitutional and political theorists. Papers were revised to reflect the intensive discussions by the group as a whole. The inquiry was crosscultural and transnational; the questions posed formed themselves across a broad spectrum of interests and knowledge, reflected in the composition of the study group. The resulting volume is a product, therefore, of expertise on important countries and regions and of authority in the theological and cultural disciplines. The ferment of the discussions was assured by the fact that the study group comprised a forum for specialists and generalists unique in the experience of many of the participants.

It remains for others to assess and evaluate the contribution of such an inquiry. The remarkable continuity of the core group attests to the value of the inquiry for members of the study group. The subject of human rights is manysided and complex, and the need for greater knowledge led one observer to call for a national or an international endowment on human rights. If the usefulness of such discussions prompts others to continue and expand the dialogue, the long-term objective of the organizers will have been served.

Special thanks for the successful completion of this project go to Philip Johnson who, as President of CRIA, oversaw the plans from the beginning; to James Finn, who was not only a member of the study group but who served as General Editor of this book; to Ulrike Klopfer, who arranged the meetings, provided logistical support, and did the yeoman work of typing the draft manuscripts; to Susan Woolfson, who did the final copyediting and typing and treated the smallest error as an evil to be eradicated.

If it were the practice to dedicate a book such as this, the dedication would read: To Randolph P. Compton who, as Chairman of the Board of the Compton Foundation, provided the funding without which the project would not have been undertaken.

Kenneth W. Thompson

vi

TABLE OF CONTENTS

CONTRIBUTORS TO THIS VOLUME

KENNETH W. THOMPSON is Commonwealth Professor of Government and Foreign Affairs at the University of Virginia and author, most recently, of *Ethics, Functionalism, and Power in International Politics*. . . *J. BRYAN HEHIR*, a Roman Catholic priest, is Associate Secretary for International Justice and Peace, U.S. Catholic Conference. . . .*ADDA B. BOZEMAN* is Professor Emeritus of International Relations at Sarah Lawrence College and an acknowledged authority on international law and the Third World. . . .*NORMAN A. GRAEBNER* is Edward R. Stettinius Professor of History at the University of Virginia. . . .*EDWARD L. KEENAN* is Professor of History and Dean of the Graduate School of Arts and Sciences at Harvard University. . . .*SHAO-CHUAN LENG* is Doherty Professor of Government and Chairman of the Asian Studies Committee at the University of Virginia. . . .*RALPH BUULTJENS*, born in Sri Lanka, teaches at the New School for Social Research, Maryknoll Graduate School, and Pace University. He is author of several books, including *Rebuilding the Temple--Tradition and Change in Modern Asia* and, most recently, *The Decline of Democracy*. . . .*ASMAROM LEGESSE*, born in Ethiopia, is Professor of Anthropology at Swarthmore College. . . .*JAMES P. PISCATORI* teaches in the Department of Government at the University of Virginia. . . .*BRIAN SMITH* is Research Associate at the Woodstock Theological Center, Georgetown University. He has completed a doctoral dissertation on the Chilean Catholic Church and Political Change, 1920-78. . . .*WILLIAM L. BRADLEY* is President of the Edward W. Hazen Foundation. He is author of *The Meaning of Christian Values Today* and has completed a manuscript on nineteenth-century Americana in Siam, in which country he taught for a period.

HUMAN RIGHTS AND U.S. FOREIGN POLICY:
A PERSPECTIVE FROM THEOLOGICAL ETHICS

J. BRYAN HEHIR

I will here use the resources of theological ethics
to examine the relationship of human rights and foreign policy. The argument will proceed in three
steps: first, perspectives on policy; second, positions on human rights; third, the ethical calculus
of human rights in foreign policy.

I. *Human Rights and Foreign Policy: Perspectives*

The normative views about the relationship of
human rights and foreign policy are sufficiently
diverse that it is necessary to survey the spectrum
of views prior to stating one's own position. The
purpose of this section is to identify in general
terms four policy perspectives, all of which will
differ from the position advocated in this essay.
The positions outlined here are normative in the
sense that they view the question of human rights as
a moral issue in the policy process; they differ
about whether the introduction of the issue will be
morally beneficial and whether it is being correctly
or sincerely included in the U.S. policy process.
The first two positions summarized here have been recurring themes in the debate about U.S. foreign
policy; the other two positions are a product of the
recent attention paid to human rights in the Carter
administration.

The first position asserts that the introduction

of human rights concerns into the policy debate is simply a new form of *moralism*. This view finds in the human rights logic and language another example of the recurring need in the American psyche and political system to cast our policy objectives in universal moral terms rather than in the more modest categories of national interest and the necessities of power.[1] If this initial perspective is valid, then the human rights arguments are vulnerable to the same "realist" critique previously made of "moralism." In essence the argument is that the pursuit of maximal moral objectives in the political process inevitably yields a style of policy which is incapable of formulating and attaining those more narrow but precise political goals that are proper to foreign policy in a decentralized international system. The moralistic posture can be both politically dangerous as well as psychologically disastrous because of the propensity to rationalize moral objectives in self-serving ways.

The second position complements the critique about moralism. It views the human rights debate as a form of *messianism* in foreign policy.[2] For those holding this position, the consequences of a strong human rights policy are to set the U.S. off on a course of pursuing unattainable objectives and/or of trying to shape other political systems in a mold they will not or cannot fit. The result will be frustration for us and potentially damaging consequences for others.

A third position holds that human rights objectives should be an explicitly defined dimension of U.S. foreign policy, not as a matter of humanitarian concern, but as an *instrument of policy*, a tactical weapon in the conflict with communism. This position sees human rights as a normative issue in world politics, but one that can be used to partisan advantage. One advocate of this position has argued

that "Concepts of human rights should be as integral
to American foreign policy as is Marxism-Leninism to
Soviet or Chinese or Yugoslav operations and planning."[3]

A fourth position is the mirror image of the
third: It holds that the human rights emphasis is
simply a *tactical camouflage* to conceal pursuit of
U.S. interests, which remain unchanged by the human
rights language.[4] This position, visible with vary-
ing degrees of intensity in Third World commentaries
on U.S. policy, reduces the human rights issue to a
new phase in a continuing strategy to keep the developing world in economic dependency while using a
language of political democracy.

The purpose of this introductory survey is not
to enter an extended debate with these four positions, although each of them could be elaborated
with a number of subordinate themes. The only response ventured here to all four is to say, "it
isn't necessarily so." To advocate a legitimate
role for human rights concerns in the policy process
does not mean that the result will be any of the
four conclusions just outlined. Each of them is a
possible product; none of them is the inevitable
product. To say this is to become responsible for
stating a different position from any of the four
on the relationship of human rights and foreign
policy. Prior to attempting this it is necessary
to see that the complexity of the human rights question lies partially within the concept of human
rights as a philosophical idea before it becomes a
policy concern.

II. *Contending Conceptions of Human Rights:
     Four Views*

The ambiguity of the role of human rights in
policy decisions does not rest solely with either

3

the delicacy of specific cases or the nature of foreign policy. Some of the roots of complexity reside in the diverse content given to the concept of human rights. Within the Western philosophical system alone it is possible to distinguish four forms of human rights discourse. Since a detailed exegesis of the four traditions is beyond the scope of this chapter, the differences will be exemplified by constructing three arguments among the contending positions. The four sources of human rights claims within the Western tradition are: the Classical Case (e.g., Cicero); the Christian Case (e.g., John XXIII); the Liberal Case (e.g., Locke); the Marxist Case (e.g., Marx). These representative figures are meant to exemplify a tradition of philosophical argument, without taking account of the pluralism that exists within each of the traditions.

A. *The Classical and Christian Positions*

The first argument is the Classical-Christian exchange about human rights and natural law. The key issue that distinguishes the two traditions is the question of transcendence. Both Cicero and Aquinas are representatives of the natural law tradition. Indeed, Cicero's presentation of the meaning of natural law appears at first glance to be substantially the same as a Christian version:

> True law is right reason in agreement with nature; it is of universal application, unchanging and everlasting....We cannot be freed from its obligations by senate or people, and we need not look outside ourselves for an expounder or interpreter of it. And there will not be different laws now and in the future, but one eternal and unchangeable law will be valid for all nations and all times, and there will be one master and ruler, that is God, over us all for he is the author of this law, its promulgator and its enforcing judge.[5]

4

The difficulty with accepting this statement of a Classical version of natural law is that it is preceded in other works of Cicero (*On the Nature of the Gods; On Divination*) by a denial of the theological truth about God and divine providence.[6] This denial presumably means that, in the Classical view, the person who is the subject of human rights exists in a closed universe. The rights of the person may be grounded in human nature which is unique in creation, but these rights are not in turn rooted in any transcendent source.

In the Christian version of natural law and human rights, the natural law argument fits securely within a framework of the order of redemption and grace. The argument about human rights is philosophical in style and substance; it is an argument that is made, as in Pope John XXIII's *Pacem in Terris* (1963), to appeal to all people of goodwill, but the roots of the argument and its ultimate development are framed in a way that opens philosophy to theology. Leo Strauss, in contrasting the position of Aquinas with that of the Classical period, argues that "the Thomistic doctrine of natural right or, more generally expressed, of natural law is free from the hesitations and ambiguities which are characteristic of the teachings, not only of Plato and Cicero, but of Aristotle as well."[7] In elaborating on this difference in the two versions of natural law, Strauss concludes that "it is reasonable to assume that these profound changes were due to the influence of the belief in biblical revelation."[8]

The significance of the influence of revelation upon the natural law-human rights argument is that it grounds the worth of the person (and therefore the rights of the person) on a qualitatively different level from an argument which cannot acknowledge a dimension of transcendence in the person.

The argument from transcendence does not erode the philosophical truth about the unique dignity of the person, but it provides this insight with a degree of conviction and content that transforms the discussion from respect for the person to reverence for the person. In contemporary Catholic teaching this fusion of both philosophical respect for the dignity of the person and religious regard for the transcendence of the person can be found by comparing the teaching of *Pacem in Terris* with that of *Gaudium et Spes* and *Dignitatis Humanae* of Vatican II.[9] *Pacem in Terris* is the clearest and most detailed natural law statement about the rights of the person in contemporary Catholic thought; the encyclical was directed to all people of goodwill, and its style of argument was open to all who would accept the tradition of reasoned debate about human rights and the political order. The argument in *Gaudium et Spes* has a different tenor and tone; it is more explicitly theological and its states the human rights case in different form. The argument from transcendence is more forthright in the conciliar document because, the council declares, "it is only in the mystery of word made flesh that the mystery of man truly becomes clear."[10] Given this premise, it is not surprising to find in *Gaudium et Spes* the view that "the dignity of man rests above all on the fact that he is called to communion with God."[11]

The declaration on religious liberty, *Dignitatis Humanae*, stands between the perspective of *Pacem in Terris* and that of *Gaudium et Spes*. On one hand the declaration, which bases its entire argument for religious liberty on the dignity of the person, clearly builds on *Pacem in Terris*. The Church seeks to explain the religious truth of freedom in reasoned terms. On the other hand the declaration spends a substantial portion of its case on "Religious Freedom in the Light of Revelation." In this chapter of the declaration the council sets forth its conviction that revelation "shows forth the dignity of the human person in all its fullness."12 In this section the *Gaudium et Spes* argument that the transcendence of the person is the ultimate meaning of human dignity is reflected and developed in terms of the specific human right of religious liberty.

The Classical-Christian argument yields not only an understanding of how two sources of the natural law argument about human rights can differ, it also yields an insight into the potential of the Christian argument on human rights. Because it is a philosophically grounded rational statement of the human rights case, as exemplified in *Pacem in Terris*, it is a position that can be allied with and open to other forms of human rights advocacy; it is not a position "imprisoned" or cut off from other positions by its faith perspective. At the same time, since it is ultimately grounded in a vision of faith and transcendence, the Christian view acquires a force and conviction that place the worth of the person in a unique setting. The transcendent destiny of each person is the ultimate truth the Christian position relies upon in its human rights advocacy. Because of that destiny, no civil power, political cause, or ideological vision can claim the right to subordinate the person to its ends. The transcendence of the person relativizes the political claims of any human institution.

B. *The Liberal-Christian Positions*

The second argument is the Liberal-Christian debate. The key issue is philosophical anthropology. Precisely, it is the question of the social nature of the person. The Liberal tradition, exemplified in Locke, uses terminology and concepts that are analogous to the Christian natural law position.

7

Beneath the shared use of terms like natural law, natural right, and human dignity, however, lies a significant difference of understanding about the person who is the subject of rights. For the Christian position, the person is social by nature; in the Lockean position, the person is social by necessity. This means that in the Christian view the person can arrive at full human development only within a social context described in terms of family, society, and state, which are "natural institutions." For the Lockean social contract position, the person is by nature self-sufficient, devoid of intrinsic social bonds or responsibilities; the person enters the framework of society and the state, not as a "natural setting" in which human development occurs through social interchange, but only because the protection of life, liberty, and property is too arduous outside some social setting.

These two fundamentally different views of the human person yield two significantly different understandings of social and political life. While both positions exhibit concern for the rights of the person, the understanding of rights is at best an analogous one, and the analogy is strained at key points. In the Lockean view, the understanding of rights is not joined with any notion of shared responsibilities. The person enters civil society with rights, but not bound by a fabric of social responsibilities. In the Christian view, rights and duties are correlative notions, both rooted in the social nature of the person. In the Lockean conception, the function of the state is to facilitate the individual exercise of his/her rights. In the Christian view, the state not only is called to facilitate the exercise of rights but also to coordinate the fulfillment of our human responsibilities in society.

The differences of the two positions are illustrated in terms of their understandings of freedom. In the Liberal position, the principal meaning of freedom is "freedom from" interference in the exercise of one's rights. In the Christian position, the deepest meaning of freedom is "freedom for" engagement with others in society. Such a depiction of the two notions of freedom is useful to highlight the divergence of the two positions. It fails, however, to indicate how, in spite of fundamental differences, there has occurred some shared understanding of the idea of freedom between the two traditions. Both the common elements and the divergent strains of the idea of rights and freedom will become clearer in the next argument.

C. *The Liberal-Marxist Positions*

The third argument within the Western tradition about human rights is the Liberal-Marxist conflict concerning rights. The key issue is one of political philosophy. Specifically, it involves the question of what one recognizes as a human right in society. The Liberal tradition is identified with and lays its stress upon civil and political rights as the human rights of the person. In his essay, "On the Jewish Question," Marx contrasted political emancipation with true human emancipation, and went on to offer his critique of the Liberal conception of rights: "Thus none of the so-called rights of men goes beyond the egoistic man, the man withdrawn into himself, his private interest and his private choice, and separated from the community as a member of civil society."[13]

In the Marxist tradition, as it has been embodied in socialist societies, rights "are social *objectives* to which the state is committed and social *means* which the state obligates itself to provide in pursuance of these material ends."[14] The difference between these two conceptions of rights, sometimes described as political-civil rights versus socio-economic rights, involves more than simply the way one classifies rights. Involved in the Liberal-Marxist argument are two fundamental differences: How should the nature of a right be defined, and how should society be structured to protect and promote human rights?

The Liberal tradition interprets a right as an immunity from coercion; a right in this sense is understood as a circle of protection within which the person is guaranteed a sphere of freedom from intervention by state power or other organized forces in society. The Marxist tradition interprets a right as an empowerment, a moral claim that the person makes on society as a whole. These two understandings of the meaning of human rights yield two distinct views of how society should be structured. The Liberal view of a right as an immunity yields a correlative notion of the limited state; the power of the state should be constitutionally contained so that it may not unjustly intrude on the rights of the person. The Marxist view of a right as an empowerment yields the correlative notion of an expansive definition of the state. While the state is ultimately destined to wither away, in the interim phase of perfecting society the state is the ultimate, perhaps the principal, agency that guarantees that each person has access to the basic social and economic goods necessary for decent existence.

The complexity of the conflict between the Liberal and Marxist positions is only symbolized by these contrasting conceptions of what constitutes a right. The contrast is sufficient, however, to highlight how the Catholic tradition on human rights intersects with these two views. If one takes *Pacem in Terris* as a contemporary statement of the Roman Catholic view, it is striking that in paragraphs 8-

27 of the encyclical Pope John affirms a spectrum of rights that encompasses both political and civil liberties and socio-economic claims.[15]   The logic of this position is to affirm a dual notion of right as both a moral immunity from unjust coercion and a moral claim for access to necessary goods. The comprehensiveness of the moral position is matched, however, by the generality of its state-ment.   There is little concrete guidance given in the encyclical as to how society is to be structured to meet the legitimate demands for freedom and jus-tice contained in the spectrum of rights affirmed.

Although not directly addressed in *Pacem in Ter-ris*, the question that lies at the root of this problem has been the subject of scrutiny in Catholic teaching.   It is the determination of the legitimate role of the state in society.   John Courtney Murray has argued that a distinct move occurred in Catholic teaching from the ethical and paternal view of the state found in Leo XIII to the more limited juridi-cal notion found in Pius XII and affirmed in *Pacem in Terris*.[16]   In this view, the state is a unique actor in society, but its functions are defined and established in constitutional terms designed to keep the state limited and accountable to the citizenry.

Accepting this definition of the state renders all the more crucial some framework for interpret-ing when state action should be contained to protect personal rights and when it should be expanded to meet unfulfilled needs.   The two parameters to be found in Catholic teaching as guidance for this question are the principle of subsidiarity elabor-ated by Pius XI in *Quadragesimo Anno* and the "prin-ciple" (really a process that requires articulation of principles) of socialization first examined by John XXIII in *Mater et Magistra*.   The subsidiarity principle functions to limit state action unless it can be shown to be necessary in the name of the

common good. Since the concept of the common good
has increasingly been defined in Catholic teaching
in personalistic terms, i.e., in terms of protecting and promoting the rights of each person, state
intervention must be justified in terms of the good
of the persons living in the society.

Pope John's discussion and evaluation of socialization functions to expand the categories of legitimate reasons for state intervention in society.
Again, while the areas of possible intervention are
multiple (economy, social relationships, culture),
the principal justifying cause for expanding state
action must be the needs of the person in society.
The concepts of subsidiarity and socialization are
best understood, I believe, as procedural rather
than substantive norms in Catholic teaching. That
is to say, they provide criteria by which to judge
the necessity or legitimacy of state action in different cases rather than providing a substantive
listing of the duties of the state. Used in tandem,
the concepts of subsidiarity and socialization will
at times call for an expansive use of state power,
and at other times they can be used to question,
criticize, or prohibit the expansion of state power.
Both the justification and the limitation of state
action will be carried out in the name of the person, and the determination of which policies and
procedures serve the good of the person will be determined principally by the spectrum of rights and
responsibilities set forth in paragraphs 8-27 of
Pacem in Terris.

The limited purpose served by constructing these
three arguments is to illustrate the complexity
that lurks beneath the surface of debates about human rights and foreign policy. The philosophical
basis of what one means by human rights is seldom
set forth in policy debate, much less the societal
model that a given conception of right entails. It

would be surprising if any one of the four traditions identified here were held today in an exclu-
sive way. The present state of the question has
gone beyond each of the individual traditions, as
is shown in Secretary Vance's 1977 Law Day address.18
At the same time, these four positions provide the
philosophical structure for much of the present debate, and it is of some interest to see that the
structure is pluralist, containing an amalgam of
views which are not easily put together in a systematic way.

III. *Human Rights and the Policy Equation*

In contrast to the sparsely developed philosophical dimension of the human rights debate, the
policy questions have been examined from several
angles. The focus of this section is to analyze
the ethical calculus by which the human rights dimension of foreign policy can be related to its
other aspects.

A. *The Setting and Substance of Policy*

The phrase "ethical calculus" is chosen purposely to convey a conviction that the inclusion of human rights considerations in foreign policy involves
a continuing process of weighing and balancing.
This conviction in turn is rooted in the basic position espoused here about the relationship of human
rights and foreign policy. The position can be
stated in two assertions: first, that human rights
are both a legitimate and a necessary consideration
in every dimension of U.S. foreign policy; second,
that the human rights concern must be woven into
the larger foreign policy equation. Both assertions
require elaboration.

There are three distinct arguments that can be
made to support the assertion that human rights are

13

a legitimate and necessary dimension of U.S. foreign policy. The legal argument is that the United States is party to international instruments like the U.N. Charter and the accompanying U.N. Declaration of Human Rights, which at least imply an obligation to assume responsibility for human rights in the international system. The historical argument is that the very sense we have of ourselves as a nation is embedded in a philosophy of rights and thus should find expression in the way we project American influence in the world. Both of these cases, the legal and the historical, admit of detailed exposition, which has been made in other places. Instead of rehearsing these arguments, the emphasis here will be placed on a third case, drawn from the nature of foreign policy today. Briefly, the human rights question should be seen today as one of the transnational problems in the international system. These questions, ranging from monetary issues through environmental controls to food and population, exhibit similar formal characteristics. They are macroquestions that cut across national boundaries, affecting large segments of the global population and reaching beyond the capacity of any single state to resolve. Yet they are of such a nature that they cannot be left unresolved. Although the human rights question does not have the same kind of impact on the daily character of foreign policy as monetary questions, it increasingly is perceived to be a central rather than an optional policy problem. Precisely because there exists no adequate international instrumentality to address the transnational issue of human rights, the burden of protecting and promoting basic rights falls upon the states, which remain the unique actors in international politics. The convergence of legal, historical, and analytical arguments establishes the presumption that human rights is an abiding element of policy today.

The presumption must be implemented by a human

rights policy. The essence of policy involves blending a mix of factors into a coherent and con-sistent pattern of action. This raises the second assertion about how human rights concerns are to be factored into the policy equation. It is pre-sumed here that human rights and foreign policy can-not be equated; the concerns of foreign policy are broader than human rights. At the same time, it is clear that an effective concern for human rights requires that it be included in principle at the very initiation of policy. If human rights objec-tives are treated as an addendum or footnote to larger political, strategic, or economic considera-tions, then the human rights factor will never sub-stantively influence policy. The policy product reflects the weight given to each factor at the very initiation of the policy process. The significant shift in human rights policy that occurred with the Carter administration was an acceptance in prin-ciple to install human rights as a constant element in the policy equation. This step makes it possible to carry on the politico-moral process of systemat-ically balancing the human rights concern against other objectives of policy. Before commenting on how this weighing of human rights should occur, it is necessary to return to the criticisms that giv-ing such a priority to human rights will lead to moralism or messianism.

Two procedural guidelines can be proposed to guard against these real pitfalls. First, the per-spective that should govern the role of human rights in foreign policy. The human rights policy should not be envisioned as a means of projecting U.S. values (i.e., pluralistic democracy) on others. Rather, human rights standards should be conceived as a self-denying ordinance on the United States. Specifically, the primary function of human rights criteria should not be to tell others what to do but to indicate to others what kinds of policies

the United States will neither aid nor abet. In
the first instance, human rights standards should
act as a restraint on U.S. policy, limiting active
cooperation with regimes that violate basic human
rights in a systematic fashion. Such a conception
of human rights standards as a self-denying ordinance on us, not a program to be foisted on
others, is a limited conception of policy designed
to avoid messianic pretensions in a very pluralistic international system.

Second, the protection against moralism resides
in the rule that the human rights objectives should
be systematically weighed against other considerations in the foreign policy equation. The presumption here is that moralism is the corruption of
moral reasoning. The antidote to moralism is
rigorous application of the standards of moral judgment. It is easier to identify these standards
(e.g., principles of generalizability, consistency,
etc.) than to apply them in the matrix of foreign
policy decisions, but this is true in any serious
issue of public morality. The manner in which the
human rights factor can be tested against other elements of policy can best be illustrated in terms of
principles and examples.

B. *The Policy Equation*

In defining the moral calculus of the human
rights policy, it is necessary at the outset to assess the pattern of relationships in which the
human rights problem emerges. The two basic relationships are the East-West and North-South questions. Looked at from the point of view of U.S.
policy, these relations vary in terms of three factors: the nature of the political relationship,
the instruments of policy and leverage available,
and the domestic constituency supporting a human
rights approach to policy.

16

The East-West problematic, exemplified by U.S.-Soviet relations, is by definition an adversary relationship. This basic characteristic means, in turn, that the instruments for U.S. influence are few (although not absent) and that the margin of movement for U.S. policy is narrow (because our leverage is limited). At the same time, domestic support for such a policy is strong. The North-South problematic, exemplified by U.S.-Latin American or U.S.-Philippine relations, is an alliance relationship. The consequences of this are that the instruments of influence are multiple and U.S. leverage, as well as U.S. involvement in the policy of the ally, is usually substantial. Domestic support for human rights policy vis-à-vis U.S. allies is less visible and more fragmented than for U.S. policy toward the Soviet Union. None of these three factors--political relationship, degree of influence, or public support--possesses explicit moral characteristics, but all shape the way in which the moral calculus is determined, since public morality involves a balancing of what *ought* to be done with what *can* be done.

To illustrate what is meant by the ethical calculus, it is possible to distinguish four general "cases" of human rights and U.S. policy. In all four cases the politico-moral balancing will be cast between human rights considerations and questions of military security. The purpose of the cases is simply to indicate how a commitment in principle to include human rights in the foreign policy equation can produce significantly different policy conclusions, each of which has its own distinctive logic and rationale.

The central case in East-West relations is the role human rights should have in pursuing U.S.-Soviet policy. Some of the commentary on human rights reduces the whole policy to this relation-

17

ship. It is the most politicized of the human
rights questions and involves the highest stakes.
Few, if any, voices in the U.S. policy debate question whether human rights should be part of the
policy with the Soviets; the hard questions arise
when the moral good of protecting human rights is
weighed against a substantial moral good like arms
control. Since the political relationship is an
adversary position between parties of commensurate
strength, the margin of leverage is narrow and the
Soviets retain the capacity to deny the United
States objectives that may affect the entire international system. To give human rights a unilateral-
ly determined value in this situation could be
morally irresponsible because of the contending
values at stake and the narrow margin of leverage
possessed by the United States in this adversary
relationship. In contrast, if the East-West case
involved trade with Czechoslovakia, a different
calculus would be at work in terms of both the contending values and the degree of influence available to the United States.

A very different kind of political and moral
equation emerges in the North-South case or in
alliance relationships. Here the posture of the
United States is fundamentally different; it is not
outside the situation seeking to influence it but
is part of the policy equation. The bonds that tie
it to the human rights situation in an allied country may be a treaty agreement, or economic or military assistance; in some way the United States is
closer to being an accomplice than an adversary.
In this different posture the problem exists of
balancing human rights claims and military or
economic assistance being provided to a government
accused of human rights violations. A more developed framework for policy judgment exists for this
problem, since Congress has passed legislation
that makes it necessary to evaluate all forms of

military and economic assistance by human rights criteria.[19] Even with this framework, however, it is necessary to see that different kinds of cases exist. Three types of security versus human rights decisions can be conceived.

The first exists when the ethical calculus should weigh in favor of the human rights factor, denying legitimacy of the security claim. This is best illustrated in Latin American cases when the government is accused by sources within and outside of gross human rights violations and yet still receives U.S. military assistance under the justification of security needs. At times the case is made that U.S. security is dependent upon the stability of the government in question or of the region as a whole. After almost fifteen years of this pattern, beginning with the Brazilian military coup in 1964 and now extending over the whole region of Central and Latin America, enough is known about the conception of security used in this argument to deny it the power to override human rights claims. In most instances the threat to "security and stability" derives from a prolonged conflict between an authoritarian military government and the civil population of the country. Such a definition of security should not qualify a government for U.S. assistance in the face of human rights claims being made against the same government. The presumption of the ethical calculus should be in favor of human rights; the burden of proof rests upon those who would argue for an overriding legitimate security requirement.

The antithetical case is a situation in which legitimate and verifiable questions of security are so dominant that human rights claims can be subordinated at least temporarily. The example that fits this model of ethical calculus is the Middle East. There are charges of human rights

19

violations made against Israel and against a number
of Arab states. Most of these states, on both
sides of the Middle East conflict, receive U.S.
military assistance. How should human rights
claims be weighed in these cases? The dominant
political and moral problem in the Middle East is
the conflict over territory, sovereignty, and
legitimacy that has convulsed the region for thirty
years. Until there is some basic resolution of
these macro-questions of politics and security the
ability to deal with human rights claims in a systematic fashion is gravely impaired. In this instance the presumption should be given to the
security questions, not because they have greater
intrinsic value than human rights claims, but because they must be resolved in order that the human rights questions can be addressed.

A third case fits between the Latin American and
Middle East examples. It involves U.S. assistance
to the Republic of South Korea. This case is perhaps the most delicate of the "North-South" issues
in the human rights debate. It is possible to
argue in the Korean case that there exists both an
authentic security question (avoiding war on the
Korean peninsula) and a human rights situation in
the South that cannot simply be subordinated to
security considerations. In the Korean case the
kind of ethical balancing that all the alliance
cases exhibit becomes very complicated. The process of evaluating what weight should be given to
human rights claims in deciding how the United
States should relate to the Park regime forces us
to examine what we mean by security. The human
rights advocates within South Korea do not deny
that an external security threat exists; but they
are convinced that the regime of authoritarian
control, devoid of respect for human rights and
democratic freedom, is in fact eroding the security
of the country by suppressing the spirit and morale

of the Korean people. These voices for human rights within South Korea ask that the security claims of the Park regime be tested critically before they are accepted as the overriding feature of our policy vision regarding their country.

Having sketched these different examples of how the human rights factor is related to other considerations of policy, it becomes clear that ethical decisionmaking on human rights cannot be a mechanical process. The phrase "ethical calculus" implies a systematic method of reflection that must go on continually within the larger foreign policy process. The intrinsic value and power of human rights claims give them a privileged place in any humane policy. But the nature of foreign policy, in the world as it is, means that the claims must be considered and pursued within a framework of other factors. The way in which we evaluate the claims and pursue policies that not only honor but move toward their achievement is the test of the moral wisdom and political vision of a human rights policy.

Notes

1. Charles Frankel, in a perceptive review of the realist critique of moralism, cites as a tenet of the critique "the belief that if people scaled down their moral demands, they might develop a foreign policy capable of accomplishing modest but decent purposes and of avoiding major disasters" ("Morality and U.S. Foreign Policy," *Worldview*, June, 1975, p. 16).

2. Ambassador George Kennan succinctly states the case: "Those Americans who profess to know with such certainty what other people want and what is good for them in the way of political institutions would do well to ask themselves whether they are not actually attempting to impose their own values, traditions and habits of thought on peoples for whom these things have no validity and no usefulness" (*The Cloud of Danger* [Boston: Little, Brown, 1977], p. 43, as quoted in Arthur Schlesinger, Jr., "Human Rights and the American Tradition, *Foreign Affairs*, 57, 3 [1979]: 517).

3. Daniel P. Moynihan, "The Politics of Human Rights," *Commentary*, August, 1977, p. 23.

4. Bolivian Permanent Assembly for Human Rights, "From National Security to Trilateralism," *LADOC*, 9 (1978): 24-39.

5. Cicero, *The Republic*, III, 23; Loeb Classical Library (Cambridge, Mass.: Harvard University Press, 1970), p. 211.

6. J. Holton, "Marcus Tullius Cicero," in *History of Political Philosophy*, eds. L. Strauss and Joseph Cropsey, 2d. ed. (Chicago: Rand McNally College Publishing Company, 1972).

7. Leo Strauss, *Natural Right and History* (Chicago: University of Chicago Press, 1953), p. 163.

8. Ibid.

9. For all three texts cf. Joseph Gremillion, *The Gospel of Peace and Justice: Catholic Social Teaching Since Pope John* (New York: Orbis, 1976).

10. Ibid., p. 260.

11. Ibid., p. 257.

12. Ibid., p. 344.

13. Karl Marx, "On the Jewish Question," in *Writings of the Young Marx on Philosophy and Society*, eds. Lloyd D. Easton and Kurt H. Guddat (New York: Doubleday, 1957), pp. 236-37.

14. Yale Task Force, "Moral Claims, Human Rights, Policies," *Theological Studies*, 35 (1974): 97.

15. Gremillion, pp. 203-206.

16. John Courtney Murray, "The Problem of Religious Freedom," *Theological Studies*, 25 (1964): 544-45.

17. Gremillion, pp. 154-56, for John XXIII's review of Pius XI's principle and his own statement of the meaning of socialization.

18. The secretary spells out three categories of rights that U.S. policy is committed to espouse; the scope of these rights cuts across the divide between political-civil and socio-economic rights, specifying also a third category of rights of the integrity of the person. "Human Rights Policy," Department of State, Bureau of Public Affairs, 30 April 1977.

19. For a review of the relevant congressional language cf. "Human Rights: Getting Through a Policy Maze," *The Congressional Quarterly*, 5 August 1978, p. 2049.

LAW, HUMAN RIGHTS, AND CULTURE

ADDA B. BOZEMAN

I.

One of the many helpful difficulties I have experienced in the course, first, of studying law,
history, and diplomacy in Europe, and later in trying to understand non-European societies, relates
to speculations about the role of ideas in shaping
civilizations. Following some of my mentors, among
them A.N. Whitehead in *Adventures of Ideas*, I am
convinced today that ideas are the major determi-
nants of human destiny in all cultures, not only
that of the West where, after Ionia and Athens, a
purely materialistic view of history is untenable,
and that differences of civilizations are best perceived by relating one's inquiries to socially and
historically prevalent thoughtways and concepts.
However, I am also certain that the life cycles of
ideas usually cannot be identified precisely, and
there there are no reliable answers to questions
such as these: How do concepts arise, change, and
die? Can the beginnings or transformations of an
idea be dated? Just when did a long familiar
notion shed its meaning, and just what is happening
to the word that carried this idea? Each of the

_____

The author is grateful to The Virginia Quarterly
Review *for permission to reproduce here excerpts
from her article,* "Law and Diplomacy in the Quest
for Peace," *which appeared in Vol. 55, No. 1.*

three concepts used in the title of this piece has a long and checkered history, and each has undergone metamorphoses and mutilations that should be diagnosed.

A second set of unresolved queries concerns the relation between culture and language on the one hand and thought and concept formation on the other. Can one maintain that thought processes in all societies are fundamentally alike when one knows that languages are greatly different? Is it safe to assume that there exists a universal common logic of thinking shared by people everywhere? Do all speech communities permit the evolution of such idea clusters as "the Categorical Imperative," "World Peace Through Law," "Self-Determination," or "Universal Human Rights"? Do the words "justice," "power," or "conflict" really evoke the same meanings and values in Iraq, Israel, Tibet, Uganda, and Canada?

The impression left by much modern literature in political science, law, and even history is indeed to the effect that perception, reasoning, analysis, and value judgment proceed under common auspices. But upon inspection these auspices turn out to be the norms of rationality, logic, and moral persuasion valid in the language worlds of the West, where the modern university with all its norm-engendering academic disciplines has its home. Situations in which the supposition of sameness cannot be substantiated readily are usually explained away with the argument that the deviation from the norm is purely temporary. Given time-- and the time concept implied here is the concept of "development"--each people *will* have a constitution, a bill of rights, and peace. The fact, well known to students of philosophy, religion, and history, that certain culturally discreet orientations toward time do not accommodate the notion of development or progress, is then conveniently dropped from consciousness, as is the widespread and un-contested knowledge that government in most parts of the world has been, and continues to be, admin-istered not in terms of law but in those of or-ganized or arbitrary power.

Visions of a unified world society have never been missing in the Christian world, but they were cultivated more cautiously and realistically in past centuries than today, and that in the realm of politics as well as in that of the academic uni-verse. Vico, for example, did not think that he could begin to fathom the unity of the human race until he had succeeded in composing a dictionary of the mental utterances common to all the nations and underlying their different languages. And Herder never tired of persuading his followers to learn difficult languages so as to explore the thought-ways of remote civilizations. More important, it cannot be said that we today lack guidelines for a more accurate appreciation of international dis-cords and accords. Dr. Robert Livingston, a well-known neurophysiologist, thus remarks that we are quite wrong in assuming the existence of a univer-sal common logic of thinking because culture, and in culture especially language, affects not only a person's values and worldviews but also the very manner in which he thinks. After all, Livingston writes, a common pool of universal thought and memory is perforce missing, since each human being has access only to a relatively uncontaminated screen of perceptional experience.[1]

Transculturally valid understandings on norms and values cannot be presumed in such circumstances. Rather, misunderstandings in international com-munications should be considered normal. Further-more, correlations or comparisons of concepts across linguistic, cultural, and ideological boundaries should be expected to be tenuous, even when accomplished philologists and translators set out to narrow the distances between thought systems.

These findings are confirmed by I.A. Richards in his work, *Mencius on the Mind*, which has the sub-title "Experiments in Multiple Definitions." The major general question here raised is the following:

How deep may differences between human minds go? If we grant that the general physiology and neurology of the Chinese and Western races are the same, might there not still be room for important psychological differences? Peoples who have lived for great periods of time in different cultural settings, developing different social structures and institutions--might they not really differ vastly in their mental constitutions?[2]

In the course of responding to these questions, Richards notes explicitly that all of us in the Occident are privileged when it comes to processes of thinking and communication because our languages derive from Greek and Latin and are based on an alphabetized script that is easily mastered. This classical Western tradition, which provides an elaborate apparatus of universals, particulars, substances, attributes, abstracts, and concretes, facilitates inventive and individuated thought. Traditional Chinese thinking, by contrast, Richards points out elsewhere,[3] gets along without the type of structure and logic we are used to. It operates within unquestioned limits, seeking a conception of the mind that should be "a good servant to the accepted moral system." Here only such conceptual distinctions are allowed as are useful in supporting social aims, and only such facts are recognized as are compatible with an approved ritual and social order. Theories of knowledge, so common in

classical and modern Western societies, were thus
not readily developed here.

Any dialogue between China and the West presupposes, in Richards's view, a close comparison of
the purposes and limitations of thought that mark
each of these two radically different civilizations. It is in this connection that he proposes a
technique for comparative studies that would establish multiple definitions of the ranges of possible
meanings carried by such pivotal terms as "knowledge," "truth," "order," "cause," or "good." However, Richards also warns that neither of these, or
other ideas, can be grasped on its merits unless
one arrives first at a reasonably reliable understanding of the entire culture in which the idea
lives.

As a student of law and history in comparative
and international contexts I am much attracted to
this type of exploration, even as I am keenly aware
of my incompetencies in the fields of linguistics
and philology. Thus it is obvious to me that any
quest for individual rights under the rule of law
is bound to be a frustrating undertaking unless we
find out just what, if anything, "individual rights"
mean in all the culturally and linguistically different societies with which we today are linked in
international relationships, and whether there is a
group of ideas resembling the one we call "law" in
the West. Gathering information about issues such
as these should be one of the main concerns not
only in scholarly circles but also, perhaps primarily, in the nation's diplomatic establishment and
in what we have come to call the intelligence community. Diplomatic investigations of this type
should be continuous, if only because ideas have a
way of changing. For example, in our relations
with China it is important to know what is traditionally Chinese about references to order, power,

conflict, peace, and war; what by contrast reflects the influence of the West, and what is distinctly Maoist in inception and usage. In respect of Maoist thought, again, it is necessary to disentangle Marxist-Leninist renditions of these crucial concepts from those that Mao derived from his ancient mentors among the Chinese martial classics.

In short, it is important in today's multicultural world to combat certain leveling dispositions that have been gaining dominance in American thought, among them the tendency to assume, without supporting evidence, that one of *our* morally preferred words and convictions carries a universally accepted truth. In the dictionary of terms relating to foreign affairs this is particularly true of "peace," "law," and, in more recent years, of "human rights."

Furthermore, it needs to be admitted that we have been careless custodians of our conceptual and linguistic heritage in the sense that we have blithely acquiesced in the wholesale pilfering and distortion of our political vocabulary. The term "people's democracy" has thus come to stand for a Communist totalitarian dictatorship, and the term "majority rule," developed in Western democracies in the context of parliamentary elections, is being used without demurrer or qualification on our part to signify the rule of black majorities over white minorities in Africa south of the Sahara, even though no one either in Africa or here envisions this kind of majority rule to be associated with constitutional proceedings. Another lost or wayward word is "imperialism." Why should we follow Lenin and apply this concept exclusively to modern, notably American, capitalism and to a brief period of European rule in parts of Africa and Asia? Why do we not remember, first, that Lenin invented the

dogma of imperialism as the last phase of capitalism
and the root cause of unjust war because he had to
find some kind of apologia or rationalization for
the nonfulfillment of Marxian prophecies; and,
second, that the annals of thousands of years of international history are replete with records of non-
European imperialisms and non-European wars?

The following reflections on law, human rights,
and culture are informed by these concerns about the
decay of our language and our conceptual apparatus,
and by the conviction that we cannot think construc-
tively about ourselves and the world environment
unless we take words and ideas seriously.

II.

The intellectual and political history of Europe and
North America establishes the fact that law has always been a paramount concern in the West. The city
states of classical Greece were poor and economical-
ly underdeveloped, but this kind of adversity did
not keep their citizens from indulging in the most
complex and advanced kind of legal and philosophical
thinking, as readers of Greek literature will readily acknowledge. Solon produced daring and successful legal reforms, and Aristotle was able to
assign meanings to equity and justice that have retained validity in our civilization to this day.
Likewise, he could analyze over a hundred different
constitutions because they evidently did exist, and
because he was intellectually ready to compare them.
The ancient Romans, meanwhile--and they too lived
in the simplest of material circumstances--developed
the most sophisticated legal system known to man.
From the fifth century B.C. onward they were relent-
lessly at work establishing categories of jurisprudence that have ever since been considered defini-
tive in the West. Public law was distinguished
from private law; the state was defined in terms of
law, and so were the rights and duties of citizens.

31

In fact nothing is quite as important for purposes of this discussion as the gradual disengagement of the autonomous person from the bonds of family and social status--a process clearly symbolized by Rome's refinement of the idea of contract.

This concept, which is the root of constitutionalism and of treaty law, presupposes the recognition that an individual is capable of having intentions of his own; that he can make and keep promises, and that he can acquire rights. After the Roman jurists had perfected these findings, they could conclude that a legally binding contract between two or more persons comes into existence when the law can isolate their authentic intentions and verify the meeting of their minds in a voluntary accord.

These intellectual breakthroughs in the private law were essential before the Romans could conceive of the constitution and of legislation as contracts in public law, and before they could describe the state as a bond or partnership in law.

All civil law societies in Christian Europe, including the Church and its canon law, carried this Roman tradition--hence the profusion of diets, synods, *cortes*, and *parlements* in the Middle Ages and the perennial concern to establish the proper relationship between power and law. In England, meanwhile, analogous emphases had evolved in the common law. Here too we find that law has traditionally had sweeping functions as a paramount moral value, a directive for thought and reasoning, a symbolic code capable of relaying other major norms and values, and as the axial principle of social behavior and political organization. The essence of civil liberties could thus be circumscribed as early as 1215, to be steadily developed in later centuries as the rights of Englishmen. What one

does not find in either of these two great legal
systems is the pretension to establish human rights
beyond the bounds of the law's actual authority and
reach. The Romans, who ended up ruling a vast empire composed of disparate cultures, speech communities, and social systems, thus did not think
that the Egyptians, for example, could be subjected
to the *ius civile* of Rome. After ascertaining the
norms and customs by which each of their depen-
dencies or satellites lived, they therefore fashion-
ed another intricate legal order, the *ius gentium*.
The English, whose nineteenth-century empire included even more diverse societies, proceeded
similarly: Wherever possible they administered their
colonies and dominions indirectly, namely, through
the agency of locally valid norms and institutions.

III.

The United States joined the European states system
as a matter of course when it gained its independence from Great Britain. However, deviations from
established norms became apparent already in the
formulation of the Declaration of Independence and
were destined to become accentuated in the first
quarter of this century, when the American government assumed the leadership of the Occidental or
transatlantic community. Among these uniquely
American orientations the following seem particularly relevant.

In light of modern elaborations of the principle
of self-determination, it is thus important to remember that this concept was affirmed in the Declaration of Independence as a universal human
right--one justifying resort to war. The great
draftsmen of this "fateful document"--as an English-
man called it--simply assumed, it seems, on the
authority of such selected European references as
the law of nature and the Lockean theory of social
contract and without analyzing the records of in-

ternational history or politics, that constitutionalism and democracy would automatically follow the
exercise of self-determination in all societies on
earth.

This confidence is very much with us today, just
as it was in the administrations of Woodrow Wilson
and Franklin D. Roosevelt--predecessors whom President Jimmy Carter cites as his models. Yet each of
the propositions that twentieth-century American
diplomacy has entrusted to the abstractions and
moral principles embodied in the eighteenth-century
document remains as controversial and unproven as
it was two hundred years ago. The concrete findings of the ancient Romans or the modern English
that "law" and "rights" cannot be presumed to em-
body or project identical meanings in the culturally disparate provinces of the world carry no weight
whatsoever in our society, perhaps because they
were registered in European empires--a type of
political organization traditionally considered
anathema in the United States. Likewise, little if
any importance is being attached to Montesquieu's
warning that the laws of one nation can never be
suited to the wants of another nation, since laws
must harmonize with the nature and the principle of
government that is established. Lastly--and oddly
enough--few today take *Professor* Woodrow Wilson
seriously when he noted in *Constitutional Government
in the United States* that

> Self-government is not a mere form of institu-
> tion to be had when desired, if only proper
> pains be taken. It is a form of character. It
> follows upon the long discipline which gives a
> people self-possession, self-mastery, the habit
> of order and peace and common counsel, and a
> reverence of law which will not fail when they
> themselves become the makers of law: the steadi-
> ness and self-control of political maturity.

And these things cannot be had without long discipline.[4]

What the nation continues to identify with are some of *President* Wilson's pronouncements, among them the following: that all states are equal even as all individuals are equal; that America must help implant a rule of justice that plays no favorites and knows no standards but the equal rights of the several peoples concerned; that diplomacy should proceed always frankly and in the public view; that the system of the balance of power has become forever discredited; that subject peoples must be granted their independence irrespective of the wishes of other states; and that war, being detested by all mankind, is everywhere susceptible to outlawry or joint international control.

Other impediments besetting the American search for world justice are related to the structure of domestic politics that allows each generation, indeed each administration, to write its own ticket in the domain of foreign affairs. This espousal of discontinuity, even impetuosity, explains, in conjunction with the strong tendency to evangelism, why we have not been able to build a philosophical base for our foreign policy, and why we do not have a time-transcendent strategic design for the furtherance of the national interest which might accommodate a realistic concern for the cause of peace with justice.

The same disabilities, in conjunction with the nation's constitutionally conditioned reluctance to recognize distinctions between civilizations, make accurate perceptions of the identities of foreign societies very difficult. The pronounced bent to see other states or peoples as actual or potential carriers of American values thus leads easily either to simplistic analogies or to unnecessarily polarized views of differences between "them" and "us." For example, in the context of our human rights diplomacy it is common to juxtapose "democracy" and "despotism" without remembering first that "democracy" is represented today by a mere handful of governments; second, that the vast majority of states, whether present or not present in the United Nations, are associated with authoritarian regimes; and, third, that there is an important systemic difference between totalitarianism as administered in the Soviet Union, Communist China, North Vietnam, Cambodia, and some of Russia's Eastern European satellites, and the kind of despotism found in most states of Latin America, the Middle East, Africa, and non-Communist Asia.

There are thus certain basic questions that American scholars and policymakers have not been in the habit of asking insistently in the last decades --decades, incidentally, during which this country had ample opportunities, by virtue of its power and unquestioned leadership in the non-Communist world, to take stock of its world environment. Among them are the following:

　　‣Can democracy or constitutionalism be expected in culture areas where the individual has not been legally detached from the group, and where the elements of contract are not accommodated?
　　‣Is it reasonable to postulate the existence of bills of rights where constitutional law is missing?
　　‣Should it be assumed that a treaty conveys the same norms and values to non-Western and Western contracting parties?
　　‣Can there be an effective international or world law if national or local meanings of public law are not analogous, or at least proximate?

If the answers to the foregoing questions are

negative, can the missing concepts be securely grafted upon public order systems built on non-legal traditions by introducing codes, constitutions, and covenants of civil liberties and by concluding international agreements assuring respect for human rights?

Answers to these and related queries cannot be given unless and until one ascertains just how societies singled out for legal transplants have been held together previously, and how strong the traditional bonds--whether derived from ritual, religion, and myth, or from military, bureaucratic, and other types of secular power--have continued to be.

Notes

1. Robert Livingston, "Perception and Commitment," *Bulletin of the Atomic Scientists*, February, 1963, p. 14.

2. I.A. Richards, *Mencius on the Mind: Experiments in Multiple Definition* (London: Routledge & Kegan Paul, 1932), p. 80.

3. C.K. Ogden and I.A. Richards, *The Meaning of Meaning* (New York: Harcourt Brace, 1959), p. 35.

4. Woodrow Wilson, *Constitutional Government in the United States* (New York and London: Columbia University Press, 1964), p. 52.

HUMAN RIGHTS AND FOREIGN POLICY:
THE HISTORIC CONNECTION

NORMAN A. GRAEBNER

I.

Behind the historic American concern for human rights lies a vision of human society formed through time by both the Judeo-Christian tradition and the affirmations of English freedom that spanned the centuries from Magna Carta to the Glorious Revolution and the Bill of Rights. These central inheritances of human society assert, in brief, that all persons possess a natural right to governments of their own consent, to equality before the law, to protection from all governmental assaults on the integrity of person, to individual conscience, and to decent and remunerative employment. Amid the economic opportunities of a rich continent and the diminishing restraints of English practice, the English settlers in the New World concluded, long before 1776, that their notions of a good society would succeed more fully in America than elsewhere. The American Revolution, as a triumphant avowal of the principles of free government, appeared to its adherents as an auspicious event in the eternal quest for human rights. Benjamin Franklin wrote for the revolutionary generation: "Establishing the liberties of America will not only make the people happy, but will have some effect in diminishing the misery of those, who in other parts of the world groan under despotism, by rendering it more circumspect, and inducing it to govern with a lighter hand."

So deeply did the French Revolution touch American liberal sentiment that when Citizen Gênet, the first minister of the French Republic, appealed to the people of Philadelphia for support, ten thousand townsmen, John Adams reported, "threatened to drag Washington out of his house and effect a revolution in the government or compel it to declare war in favor of the French and against England." Only an epidemic of yellow fever in Philadelphia saved the young American government. Thereafter the concept of a special American mission to humanity seemed to keep pace with the nation's growth. In his farewell exhortation Andrew Jackson admonished the American people: "Providence has showered on this favored land blessings without number, and has chosen you as the guardians of freedom, to preserve it for the benefit of the human race." Amid the collapse of Europe's liberal revolutions at mid-century, Lewis Cass of Michigan looked forward to a better day. "I trust the time will come," he told a New York audience, "when not a hostile drum shall roll, and not a hostile cannon be fired, throughout the world, if we say, 'Your cause is not a just or right one.'"

This sense of mission drove President William McKinley toward the annexation of the Philippines in 1898. During his October speaking tour of the Midwest he advised his listeners at Columbus, Ohio: "We know what our country is now in its territory, but we do not know what it may be in the near future. But whatever it is, whatever obligation shall justly come from this humanity, we must take up and perform, and as free, strong, brave people, accept the trust which civilization puts upon us." As catastrophe came to Europe in July, 1914, Woodrow Wilson looked forward to the time when "America will come into the full light of day when all shall know that she puts human rights above all other rights, and that her flag is the flag not only

of America, but of humanity." It was not strange
that Americans viewed all pre-1914 liberal revolutions as a vindication of this nation's revolutionary tradition and its governmental principles.
Thomas Jefferson once commented, with considerable
truth, that "the disease of liberty is catching."

Despite their obvious appeal, such references to
mission collided with another American tradition,
far more significant and pervading, which determined the actual foreign policies that the United
States pursued. George Washington's administration
established the course of America's world relationships when it refused to commit the power of the
United States to France's revolutionary cause.
Washington advised his countrymen, in matters of
foreign policy, to consult no more than the permanent interests of their country. He declared
that "it is a maxim, founded on the universal experience of mankind, that no nation is to be trust-
ed further than it is bound by its interest; and no
prudent statesman or politician will venture to de-
part from it." Again, in his Farewell Address,
Washington warned the Republic: "The nation which
indulges toward another an habitual hatred or an
habitual fondness is in some degree a slave. It is
a slave to its animosity or to its affection,
either of which is sufficient to lead it astray
from its duty and its interest."

Throughout the next century every suggestion
that the United States embark on a foreign crusade
in behalf of freedom faced the vociferous and controlling opposition of American conservatives, who
denied that the United States carried any special
obligation for humanity. In 1821, Turkish atrocities sent the Greeks into revolt. Immediately,
Americans entered a crusade to aid the Greek cause.
President James Monroe, under the close guidance
of Secretary of State John Quincy Adams, refrained

41

from issuing any declaration in behalf of the Greeks. In his oration of July 4, 1821, Adams averred that the country would always sympathize with the cause of liberty. But, he added,

she goes not abroad, in search of monsters to destroy. She is the well-wisher to the freedom and independence of all. She is the champion and vindicator only of her own....She well knows that by evaluating others under banners other than her own, were they even banners of...independence, she would involve herself beyond her power of extrication, in all the...interests and intrigue[s] [of others]. The fundamental maxims of her policy would insensibly change from liberty to force...[and] she might become dictress of the world. She would no longer be ruler of her own spirit.

During the debates on American policy toward the Greek Revolution in January, 1824, John Randolph of Roanoke asked the Speaker of the House:

Are we, sir, to go on a crusade in another hemisphere, for the propagation of two objects as dear and delightful to my heart as to that of any gentleman in this or any other assembly--Liberty and Religion--and in the name of these holy words--by this powerful spell, is this nation to be conjured and beguiled out of the high way of heaven--out of its present comparatively happy state, into all the disastrous conflicts arising from the policy of the European powers, with all the consequences which flow from them?

When President James K. Polk, in December, 1845, attempted to universalize the American interest in the Western Hemisphere under the guise of the Monroe Doctrine, the conservative John C. Calhoun argued in the Senate that the ends of policy be calculated by the means available. It was, he said, "the part of wisdom to select wise ends in a wise manner. No wise man, with a full understanding of the subject, could pledge himself, by declaration, to do that which was beyond the power of execution, and without mature reflection as to the consequences. There would be no dignity in it. True dignity consists in making no declaration which we are not prepared to maintain. If we make the declaration, we ought to be prepared to carry it into effect against all opposition."

For such nineteenth-century idealists as Jefferson, James Madison, Henry Clay, and Abraham Lincoln the United States was no more than an example-setter for the world. They were less concerned with American involvement in revolutions abroad than with the creation of a society in America that was worthy of emulation. For Jefferson, writing from Paris in 1787, the United States afforded a "primitive and precious model of what is to change the condition of man over the globe." Similarly, Alexander Smyth of Virginia reminded his fellow congressmen during the Greek debates of 1824: "The cause of freedom, the hope of mankind, depends on the ultimate success of the hitherto successful experiment in the science of government, now making in the United States. When we consider the importance of the interests confided to us, it must appear unpardonable wantonly to hazard the success of that experiment." In denying the existence of any American interest in the Polish rebellion of 1863, Secretary of State William H. Seward reminded Europe's leaders: "In view of the location of this Republic, the character, habits, and sentiments of its constituent parts, and especially its complex yet unique and very popular Constitution, the American people must be content to recommend the cause of human progress by the wisdom with which they should exercise the powers of self-government,

forbearing at all times, and in every way, from foreign alliances, intervention, and interference."
For Lincoln that year it was essential that the
Union triumph so that liberty--the heritage of all
men--would not perish from the earth.

Without exception, those who prior to McKinley
demanded American involvements abroad in behalf of
humanity were not in positions of power and responsibility. Never did they succeed in framing
policies that might secure their interests in liberation. In fact they never tried. In their total
neglect of means they demonstrated their greater
concern for popularity at home than for the cause of
liberty abroad. At no time did the liberal revolutions of Europe and Asia before 1914 elicit any
support from American external policy. Their causes,
successes, and failures hinged on conditions purely
indigenous.

II.

Before the Great War of 1914, American expressions
of idealism focused only on the benefits that freedom might bring to others. Under Wilson, however,
that moral concern, by serving as the foundation of
a new world order of peace and stability, would advance the interests of Britain, France, and the
United States above all others. The assumption
that democratic governments were peaceful and thus
would uphold the order of power that the war
created, identified American purpose with both the
universalization of democracy and the institutionalization of the international peace structure. Historically, American ideals and American interests
had coincided; thus the pursuit of interests, except perhaps for the Mexican War, did not challenge
the nation's concern for justice. But Wilson asserted that principles, not interests, should
control. This denied diplomacy, a political and
pragmatic act, a rightful role in international

affairs, for a nation could not properly compromise a legal or moral right. By denying the primacy of interests in the conduct of foreign relations, Wilson eliminated the need for ranking the country's external concerns in the order of their political and military importance. What mattered to Wilson was less the country's purposes abroad than the example for democracy and peaceful behavior that the United States offered to an undemocratic and war-torn world. Aside from his preference for democratic institutions, Wilson had little interest in human rights. At Versailles he refused to touch the Japanese-sponsored issue of racial equality; nor would he apply his own principle of self-determination to the peoples of the victorious empires.

Throughout the interwar years the followers of Wilson stressed the principle of peaceful change to the exclusion of human rights. Every program they fostered during the Twenties--membership in the League of Nations and the World Court, the resort to arbitration and conciliation, collective security, naval limitation, or the outlawry of war--was a further effort to institutionalize the peace and a denial of the need for any precise definition of either the ends or the means of national policy. American leaders, both Republican and Democrat, identified human rights with democracy, and democracy with peace. The concept of peaceful change became the bulwark of the status quo, for change limited to general agreement could alter the international order only on questions of little or no consequence. During the Thirties American politicians and journalists condemned the aggressors, not for their infringements on human rights, but for their disturbance of the peace.

It was only when the United States moved toward the use of power in 1941 that Franklin D. Roosevelt, in response to both the aggressions of the Axis powers and their repressions of domestic freedom, again established a direct relationship between the nation's search for peace and its concern for human rights. He embodied his objectives in his Four Freedoms of January, 1941, as well as in the Atlantic Charter, signed at his meeting with Winston Churchill at Placentia Bay in August. Following the Japanese attack on Pearl Harbor in December, Roosevelt explained his purposes to the American people: "We are fighting in defense of principles of law and order and justice, against an effort of unprecedented ferocity to overthrow those principles and to impose upon humanity a regime of ruthless domination by unrestricted and arbitrary force." In large measure the interests and the principles converged, as they did in 1917, but the interests and the principles were not synonymous. If the defeat of Germany and Japan served the nation's interests, it did not guarantee the triumph of its principles.

Following another war that unleashed hopes for an improving future for mankind, American leaders again identified the establishment of international peace and stability with the expansion of freedom and human rights. President Harry Truman accepted the connection between the two ideals in his address before the closing session of the United Nations conference at San Francisco in June, 1945. "The Charter," he declared, "is dedicated to the achievement and observation of human rights and fundamental freedoms. Unless we can attain those objectives for all men and women everywhere--without regard to race, language, or religion--we cannot have permanent peace and security." The United Nations Charter, in Articles 55 and 56, committed all members to promote both peace and human rights. The international movement for human rights culminated in the Universal Declaration of Human Rights, approved by the General Assembly on December 10, 1948, by a vote of 48 to 0. The eight abstentions came

from Yugoslavia, Saudi Arabia, the Union of South Africa, and five voting members of the Soviet bloc.
Again the Declaration noted the relationship between
future peace and the expansion of human rights. It
observed that "the equal and undeniable rights of
all members of the human family is the foundation of
freedom, justice and peace in the world."

Speaking before the Political Committee of the
United Nations in April, 1949, Benjamin V. Cohen repeated the common effort to create a universal interest in human rights. "Unless a state allows freedom
for the peaceful expression of ideas," he warned,
"the road toward peaceful change and progress is
blocked." Similarly, President Truman informed a
New York audience in October of that year: "We believe strongly that the attainment of basic civil
and political rights for men and women everywhere--
without regard to race, language or religion--is essential to the peace we are seeking." President
Lyndon B. Johnson, on October 11, 1967, issued a
proclamation designating 1968 as Human Rights Year
in honor of the twentieth anniversary of the Universal Declaration of Human Rights. "Governments
which systematically disregard the rights of their
own people," he said, "are not likely to respect the
rights of other nations and other people and are
likely to seek their objectives by coercion and
force in the international field." President John F.
Kennedy observed in his noted American University
address of June 10, 1963: "And is not peace, in the
last analysis, basically a matter of human rights?"

Throughout the cold war, and continuing through
the war in Vietnam, American officials assumed that
Communist totalitarianism comprised the primary danger to both world peace and human rights. Secretary
of State John Foster Dulles, ignoring the failure
of human rights among many of the country's Third
World allies, accused only Soviet and Chinese rulers

47

of trampling on moral law in their repression of
others and endangering world peace in like measure.
The Kennedy administration was less strident in its
denunciations of Moscow and Peking, but it remained
deeply committed to the principle of self-determination in its opposition to Soviet political influence
in Eastern Europe. To Secretary of State Dean Rusk
the United States fought the Communists in Vietnam
to create a world in which human rights would be
secure--a world of independent nations free to co-
operate with one another in building a free and
peaceful world. United States policy toward international communism, Rusk asserted, was "to encourage
evolution within the Communist world toward national
independence, peaceful cooperation, and open societies." The eventual retreat of Communist power,
in short, assured the triumph of peace *and* freedom
in both the Communist and the non-Communist worlds.

III.

This persistent assumption that peace and human
rights would succeed together found no verification
in the postwar experience. The widespread denial
of human rights did not disturb the general peace;
nor did it account for the wars that occurred. It
was not strange, therefore, that human rights remained near the bottom of the hierarchy of national
objectives. So negligible was the American interest
in human rights abroad that it dared not resort to
threats of violence in their pursuit. For that
reason Dulles's pronouncements on the eventual
liberation of those behind the Iron Curtain would,
in the event of a revolt, produce only embarrass-
ment at home and disillusionment abroad. The Hun-
garians should have known, despite Dulles's repeated
assurances, that the United States had no interest
in Hungarian freedom commensurate with the risk of
open conflict with the USSR. If this country could
not rescue Louis Kossuth and his Hungarian freedom
fighters from their Russian enemies in 1849, it

would not act in 1956. Dulles's perennial failure
to create policies that had some clear relationship
to his declared purposes undermined the seriousness
of his intent. Objectives that threaten the
stability of other governments either mean nothing
or they mean war. Because they generally mean nothing, they produce cynicism among those who take the
statements seriously.

As president, Richard M. Nixon recognized the
limitations that power placed on principles. In
emphasizing the need for negotiation, he proclaimed
that interests, not principles, would determine his
external policies. "We are not involved in the
world because we have commitments," Nixon declared,
"we have commitments because we are involved. Our
interests must shape our commitments rather than
the other way around." Viewing the Soviet Union as
a normal power, and thus another element in the
world's peace structure, Nixon, supported by advisor Henry A. Kissinger, was willing to recognize
Soviet primacy in Eastern Europe. Elsewhere, the
Nixon administration refused to compromise its in-
herited cold war objectives, for the further expansion of Soviet influence appeared to it a threat to
both American security and international stability.
What mattered to Nixon and Kissinger was that the
USSR join the United States in recognizing the same
rules of international conduct, that both accept
the legitimacy of the existing international order
and refrain from efforts to change it through force.
But if the rules of international conduct began
with the recognition of the sovereign rights of all
nations, they left little room for making effective
any concern for the manner in which other governments treated their citizens. Policies designed to
encourage the expansion of human rights abroad were,
by such standards, both illegitimate and nonessential.

For Nixon and Kissinger, the quality of regimes

in Asia, Africa, and Latin America that the United
States supported was immaterial. On July 25, 1974,
Kissinger testified before the Senate Appropriations
Committee: "Where we believe the national interest
is at stake we proceed even when we do not approve
{of a country's policies}." Until the final collapse of South Vietnam and Cambodia in 1975 the
United States asked nothing of their governments except that they continue to fight the Communist
enemy. In February, 1976, Kissinger signed an
agreement with Brazil on economic and political consultation without raising the subject of specific
human rights violations in that country. Chile's
military regime, despite its widely publicized repressions, continued under Kissinger to receive
more aid from the United States than any other Latin
American country. To counter his critics, who argued that American foreign policy had lost its humanitarian tradition, Kissinger, during his final
months in office, turned more and more to questions
of human rights and Third World interests, admit-
ting on occasion that "America cannot be true to itself without moral purpose." To the end, however,
he warned that American influence in a fundamentally
stable world was exceedingly limited. Congress encouraged the changing mood with legislation of its
own. The Foreign Assistance Act of 1974 restricted
the use of foreign aid to the encouragement of
"democratic private and local government institutions" in recipient states. Again, in the Foreign
Assistance Act of 1976, Congress declared: "A principal goal of the foreign policy of the United
States is to promote the universal observance of
internationally recognized human rights by all
countries."

IV.

Jimmy Carter caught this burgeoning interest in human rights on the upswing. As president after
January, 1977, he accepted the dual challenge of

rebuilding the country's reputation abroad (under the assumption that it needed rebuilding) and of creating a post-Vietnam consensus that would restore the primacy of the White House in the area of foreign affairs. To achieve both goals the Carter administration hoped to construct its new foreign policy consensus around the two large groups whom Henry Kissinger had alienated: the liberals, who objected to the former secretary's amoral realism and the cynicism he had displayed toward the repressive behavior of certain countries aligned with the United States, and the hard-liners, who believed that Kissinger had given up too much to the Russians in his quest for détente. Carter understood that the failures in Indochina, with the widespread questioning of American wisdom and purpose at home and abroad, would not be dispelled merely by declaring the war over. Nor would the effort to forget restore the president's authority in foreign affairs. Perhaps a confession or a debate might have cleared the air, but for Carter, as for Kissinger, neither course was a political possibility. It seemed far easier and less divisive to leave Vietnam to the historians and proceed with the redemption of the rest of the world. Rather than permit the United States to retreat from Vietnam into a world of power and conflict, he would reestablish the country's moral leadership. For Carter the issue that above all others would build the needed consensus and create an American role which, in the words of Vice-President Walter Mondale, would leave the American people "feeling good" was that of human rights. For Carter the issue was ideal; whereas it would permit him to reassert American leadership abroad, its pursuit would require neither a heavy expenditure of money nor an intricate and taxing foreign policy.

Carter's human rights campaign began early. "Because we are free," he declared in his inaugural address, "we can never be indifferent to the fate of freedom elsewhere." Carter reminded the permanent representatives of the U.N. on March 17, 1977: "{N}o member of the United Nations can claim that mistreatment of its citizens is solely its own business. Equally, no member can avoid its responsibilities to review and to speak when torture or unwarranted deprivation occurs in any part of the world." Carter's speech at the University of Notre Dame on May 22, 1977, entitled "A Foreign Policy Based on America's Essential Character," comprised for him a major effort to define a conceptual approach to America's new global role. Again the president promised that the nation's actions overseas would reflect the country's historic character. "I believe," he said, "we can have a foreign policy that is democratic, that is based on fundamental values, and that uses power and influence which we have for humane purposes." Democracy's example, he declared, would be compelling. Beyond that the nation would seek to inspire, to persuade, and to lead. The president condemned the "intellectual and moral poverty" of the nation's failure in Vietnam, but he insisted that "a politically awakened world" again looked to the United States for direction. For the United States to ignore the worldwide trend toward human progress, he warned, "would be to lose influence and moral authority in the world. To lead it will be to regain the moral stature we once had." Not since the time of Woodrow Wilson had the United States, or any country, staked out such hopes for humanity. How the new president intended to triumph where Wilson had failed was not clear.

Carter's program began with the restructuring of the State Department to serve the administration's humanitarian purposes. At the core of the human rights endeavor was the State Department's Bureau of Human Rights and Humanitarian Affairs, headed by

Patricia Derian, a former civil rights activist. In addition, the administration created the Interagency Group on Human Rights and Foreign Assistance, chaired by Deputy Secretary of State Warren Christopher. From the beginning Derian was determined to make the United States the conscience of the non-Communist world. Under her prodding--and that of others--the president issued a secret directive in February, 1978, which ordered all agencies to consider the impact of their decisions on the status of human rights abroad. State Department officials used every occasion to stress the importance of human rights under the assumption that words and ideas have a power of their own. The government, meanwhile, undertook diplomatic initiatives to encourage countries to release political prisoners; it reduced or halted economic assistance programs to countries engaged in serious violations, or altered such programs to benefit people rather than ruling élites; it instructed its representatives in international lending agencies, such as the Asian Development Bank, to vote against loans to repressive regimes; it worked to strengthen the Inter-American Commission on Human Rights as well as the human rights activities of the United Nations; and, finally, it supported governments that demonstrated positive efforts to improve human rights in their countries.

From time to time administration spokesmen enumerated the human rights that concerned them. The first category included personal rights, such as freedom from torture, cruel and degrading treatment, arbitrary arrest and imprisonment, the denial of a fair public trial, and invasion of the home. The second category involved the right to such necessities as food, shelter, health care, and education. The third comprised civil and personal liberties--freedom of thought, religion, assembly, speech, and press, as well as freedom of movement and freedom to participate in government. What disturbed some critics was the administration's failure to distinguish between repression and the absence of self-government in other countries. Samuel Pisar, writing in the *New York Times* of September 25, 1977, condemned the tendency to identify United States purpose abroad with the universalization of democratic values and practices:

> The posture that our new policy makers have struck toward the world conjures up the image of Don Quixote charging at windmills. It is one thing to speak out, in the name of America, against the systematic use of torture and brutality by repressive regimes, some of them in our own backyard. But to go further and urge our own political values and traditions on other nations, from China to Brazil and from Pakistan to Cuba, while the bulk of humanity is still groping for the right to work, housing, education and decent medical care, calls for extraordinary faith in the power of persuasion.

Societies at different stages of development require vastly different institutions for survival and progress. Governing, as George F. Kennan has noted, is not a moral exercise; it is a practical function to maintain order and collective discipline in the interest of social stability. Free government requires specific environmental conditions that affect only a small portion of mankind. For the bulk of humanity, economic and personal security are more important than democratic institutions. Why some countries pursued social and economic progress at the price of political freedom is obvious enough. What comprised human rights in Islamic, Oriental, and African societies, except for the absence of murder and torture, often defied definition. Many Western procedural safeguards for the defense of individual rights have no tradition

54

in many parts of the world where geography and culture preclude the establishment of full-fledged democratic institutions. Thus it was not strange that Washington had difficulty in differentiating among programs that were impossible, possible, or merely desirable. The administration's Interagency Group approved health projects for countries with repressive governments as a legitimate effort in behalf of human rights; it refused to approve aid for left-wing countries that favored economic progress to democratic procedures. Yet where, except in such countries as India, could human rights in Asia and Africa be measured by the standard of political freedom? There was little relationship between most human rights that the administration advocated and the possibility of their achievement anywhere in the Third World.

Whatever the goals of Carter's human rights crusade--and they were never articulated in specific terms--this crusade, like all crusades, would remain divorced from policy wherever repression existed outside the areas of direct American influence. "Human rights is the most complicated foreign-policy question before the government," declared one State Department official. "No one knows what the policy is, yet it pervades everything we do." Critics agreed that the president's statements lacked a systematic analysis of either American intentions or the means available for pursuing them. Obviously, no member of the Carter administration advocated military invasion or the overthrow of governments. Economic pressures could increase rather than diminish the extent of human misery in a country. Even when ineffective they could inaugurate charges that the United States was interfering in another people's national affairs. How merely criticizing another government would modify its behavior was not clear. Indeed, moral condemnation could easily cause a regime to avoid reforms to convince the world that it was not acceding to external pressure. No government would ever admit that it was immoral; nor would it agree that its behavior exceeded the bounds of necessity. President Kennedy's Alliance for Progress demonstrated that no ruling élite would adopt reforms that endangered its authority simply to obtain aid or quiet the accusations of others. There existed, finally, the risk of humiliation in declaring objectives that had no relationship to the contemplated actions of government. Kissinger reminded the Carter administration in April, 1978: "If a nation constantly affirms human rights and then does not try to carry through with the ideals in policy, it can be regarded not as strength but as impotence." Public declarations antagonize governments, arouse the hopes of the oppressed, and fuel the fervor of reformers--none of which serves any American interest.

What separated Carter from his predecessors in his attitudes toward human rights in the smaller countries was his conviction that they contributed little to the global balance between East and West. "Being confident of our own future," the president declared at Notre Dame, "we are now free of that inordinate fear of communism which once led us to embrace any dictator who joined in that fear." This revolution in the official American outlook toward communism effected profound changes in the country's policies. For Carter, Latin America presented a special problem. As late as 1963 military dictatorships controlled only four small Latin American countries--El Salvador, Honduras, Nicaragua, and Paraguay. But Brazil fell to a military junta in 1964, Panama and Peru in 1968, Bolivia in 1969, Ecuador in 1972, Chile and Uruguay in 1973, and Argentina in 1976. Behind most of these military dictatorships were officers who had trained either in United States military schools or in the Pentagon's School for the Americas, located in the Panama Canal Zone. Most of these officers had strong personal ties to high-ranking Pentagon officials. Under the Nixon-Kissinger foreign policy these dictatorships, despite their known reliance on terrorism and torture, flourished with American aid. What mattered was simply their commitment to anti-communism.

When Washington accompanied its 1977 offer of $50 million in military aid to Brazil with the State Department's report on the status of human rights in that country, the Brazilian Government announced that it would reject the offer. Such matters as human rights, it reminded Washington, remained within the exclusive competence of Brazilian authorities. Argentina, Uruguay, El Salvador, and Guatemala followed Brazil's lead. Together these countries, angered by Carter's outspoken human rights statements, rejected credits totaling $74 million. That aid in the past had scarcely served any security interests of the United States. Now Pentagon officials, freed of their former anti-Communist restraints, informed Latin American governments that their behavior on human rights would determine future military relations between the United States and their countries. The president's decision to separate the White House from the repressive regimes of Latin America quickly created a new relationship. Elio Gaspari, the Brazilian journalist, noted the change: "From the moment Latin Americans, Africans and Asians started looking at President Carter as a politician interested in human rights, the United States Embassy ceased being seen by thousands of third-world liberals as a headquarters for conservative maneuvers; it became identified with the nation it represents." Under Carter the United States was no longer the unconditional supporter of dictators and dictatorships as it had been under previous administrations. "For the last several years," noted Gaspari, "citizens of

the third world couldn't quite understand why so
many poisonous mushrooms grew in the shadow of the
American foreign policy. Today, it is the mushrooms that do not realize that the shadow is gone."
Unfortunately, the governments of Latin America
still possessed the instruments of oppression, whatever the divisions and animosities their refusal to
grant reform and democracy might create. If the
new United States-Latin American relationship
eliminated some useless and costly military expendi-
tures, it comprised no immediate triumph for human
rights.

V.

Few questioned the president's sincerity, but some
wondered about his humility and sense of proportion.
Robert McGeehan, writing in the July, 1977, issue
of the *World Today*, declared that Carter's "of-
ficious response to human rights violations abroad
...led some to wonder just how many countries he
wanted to govern." How did the president, others
asked, intend to reconcile his idealistic goals,
which concerned the internal conditions of other
countries, with the more traditional requirements
of foreign policy? "I am not cynical enough to say
that to have a good policy you cannot have *des bons
sentiments*," admitted French critic Raymond Aron,
"but I would say that it is not enough to be a
statesman to wish the best for everybody." Secretary of State Cyrus Vance recognized the limitations of any human rights policy in his address
before the University of Georgia Law School in April,
1977. United States objectives, he said, would of
necessity be circumscribed by the willingness of
other governments to tolerate outside investigation,
by the prospects of effective action, and by the
realization that violence could result in a loss
instead of a gain for human rights. Vance warned
his listeners against expecting too much of words.
"[I]n pursuing a human rights policy," he said, "we

must always keep in mind the limits of our power and of our wisdom. A sure formula for defeat of our goals would be a rigid, hubristic attempt to impose our values on others." Similarly, in May, Carter admonished his Notre Dame audience that the United States would not conduct its foreign policy "by rigid moral maxims. We live in a world that is imperfect, and which will always be imperfect....I understand fully," he added, "the limits of moral suasion." Such admissions of limited influence almost explained away the entire human rights program.

If a generalized response to human rights violations exceeded the possibilities of policy formulation, a selective response invited charges of hypocrisy. In practice the administration trimmed repeatedly when its declared purposes abroad conflicted with the country's economic and security interests. Even as the proclamations on human rights proliferated in Washington, the administration refused to indict countries whose cooperation appeared essential for reasons of trade and security. Whatever the quality of the regimes of South Korea and the Philippines, American security interests and military requirements rendered both governments too important to permit Washington the luxury of altering its military relationships with them. That the shah of Iran ran a repressive regime was well known in Washington, but the United States required Iranian oil, investments, and economic collaboration. During his trip of late March, 1978, to Venezuela, Brazil, Nigeria, and Liberia the president openly conferred with liberal critics of the Brazilian regime, but he carefully avoided any attacks on human rights violations in Africa. Carter had no desire to interfere with the efforts of his ambassador to the United Nations, Andrew Young, to court black Africa at any price.

Richard H. Ullman argued in *Foreign Affairs* of

April, 1978, that an American boycott of Ugandan coffee might compel changes in the domestic policies of that country and perhaps drive the genocidal Idi Amin from power. The Carter administration deplored the human rights violations in Uganda but argued that products barred from this country would find ready markets elsewhere. Washington officials explained, moreover, that the principles of the General Agreement on Trade and Tariffs (GATT) held the higher priority. Still, in October, 1978, the president acceded to the growing pressure around him and terminated American trade with Uganda. The Carter administration, no less than others, carried a far greater obligation to political, economic, and strategic considerations than to human rights in the formulation of policy. Secretary Vance reminded the Senate Foreign Operations Subcommittee as early as February, 1977: "In each case we must balance a political concern for human rights against economic and security goals. No formula can resolve the larger conflict of commitments...." Still, the daily necessity of elevating interests above ideals when the administration repeatedly declared human rights the essence of policy carried a heavy price. As one State Department official declared: "I see as a principal pitfall that there will be disappointment, or even cynicism, when it becomes clear we can't accomplish miracles, or, more important, when human rights doesn't seem to be the most important or overriding factor in our foreign policy."

Some Americans warned that even the appearance of an intention to link the normalization of United States relations with the USSR to changes in the Soviet system would endanger any progress toward an arms agreement. Certainly, they insisted, the military rivalry between the United States and the Soviet Union was the world's most expensive and potentially disastrous problem. Yet, during its first weeks in office, the Carter administration issued statements criticizing the governments of Russia and Czechoslovakia for harassing and intimidating citizens who attempted to exercise their right of protest. Vance instructed the Kremlin that the United States would "vigorously pursue human rights matters" that came under the East-West Helsinki Accord of 1975. In February, 1977, Carter responded to a letter from the noted Russian dissident and Nobel Peace Prize winner, Andrei Sakharov, with a letter of his own. His message of February 5, cast in general terms, declared that "human rights is a central concern of my administration....The American people and our government will continue our firm commitment to promote respect for human rights not only in our country but also abroad." The president left the matter of the letter's release to Sakharov's discretion. During March, Carter welcomed Soviet dissident Vladimir Bukovsky to the White House, breaking with President Gerald Ford's decision not to receive Aleksandr Solzhenitsyn.

Soviet leaders expressed anger at Carter's statements on human rights. What disturbed them especially were the president's references to the human rights pronouncements of the Helsinki Accord. Georgi Arbatov, head of the Soviet Institute of U.S. Studies, sounded the alarm. He reminded the administration that there were many unsettled issues in Soviet-American relations of greater importance than human rights. Such warnings were not without effect. Some American analysts complained that President Carter threatened to undo the major achievement of the Nixon-Kissinger era--the elimination of ideology from the Soviet-American relationship so that the two countries could deal in terms of their common and conflicting interests alone. Vance insisted that the administration would divorce the issue of human rights from its efforts to reach substantive agreements with the

61

Soviet Union; each question, he assured newsmen, would be discussed on its own merits. It was not clear that the Kremlin would acknowledge such a separation.

Why Washington's pronouncements in behalf of Soviet dissidents would provoke determined Soviet resistance was obvious from the beginning. Marshall Shulman, Carter's key advisor on Soviet affairs, warned a Senate committee in 1974 that any United States effort to improve human rights in the USSR would pose "conditions which the present Soviet regime cannot but regard as terms of surrender and of self-liquidation." Similarly, National Security Advisor Zbigniew Brzezinski, whose writings had never revealed much sympathy for the Soviet Union, admitted that even "a limited democratization of the Soviet society...would threaten the present political leadership." Any growth of intellectual dissent or nationalism within the Soviet Union, Brzezinski acknowledged, endangered the existence of the Soviet regime.

Against such political realities Carter's preachments had no chance. During the autumn of 1977 the president selected Arthur Goldberg to represent the administration at the Belgrade Conference, called to review compliance with the Helsinki Accord and its human rights provisions for Eastern Europe. Goldberg could find no leverage to overcome Soviet opposition to another all-European human rights resolution. The Common Market group, concerned with the status of East-West relations, displayed no interest in human rights at all. Whatever criticism of human rights violations occurred at Belgrade focused on only three countries--the Soviet Union, Czechoslovakia, and East Germany. The United States had no interest in damaging its relations with Poland, Hungary, and Rumania. The final Belgrade report contained no statement on human rights. The Carter human rights crusade, moreover, produced no apparent relaxation of Soviet emigration restrictions. Late in December, 1977, the *New York Times* noted that the Soviet human rights movement was at its lowest ebb in years.

In July, 1978, the widely publicized trial of Soviet dissident leader Anatoli Shcharansky, which concluded with his conviction and sentencing to thirteen years in a hard-labor camp, created a storm of protest throughout the world. Undoubtedly, the reaction itself comprised a major gain for human rights. "The publicity given the trials is very encouraging," observed Valentin Turchin, a Russian computer scientist and activist residing in the United States. "The awful thing about the Stalin era was that people just disappeared....Now there is public reaction, and people understand what is happening. The struggle is worth the effort." Still, the apparent ineffectiveness of American appeals to the Kremlin created a bitter mood in Washington. Senator Jacob Javits of New York took the lead in denouncing the Soviet action. He called the trial "an international disgrace" and wondered whether the free world would "succumb to the forces of evil, the forces of darkness, the forces of terror." Noting the limits of American authority, House Speaker Thomas O'Neill of Massachusetts retorted, "I don't know what we can do other than express our deep concern, regret, and displeasure." "There is no way," echoed Senator Mike Gravel of Alaska, "we're going to make them knuckle down on an internal matter." Congressman Dante Fascell of Florida reminded the American people that the trial was less important than Soviet relations with the United States.

That disturbing conflict between principle and policy pervaded the country's response to the Shcharansky conviction. President Carter's obser-

vations on the trial recognized the dilemma to
which the human rights issue had consigned the administration. "We have a deep commitment to human
rights," he said, "not only here but around the
world." Then he added quickly: "I have not embarked on a vendetta against the Soviet Union. We
cannot interfere in their internal affairs." At
Berlin, in July, the president again fell into a
trap of his own making. He told a cheering
audience: "No matter what happens, Berlin will remain free." Later, at a town meeting, he faced an
elderly woman who asked, "Can you tell us how long
we will have to live with the wall?" The president's
response was candid: "I don't know. I can't give
you a better answer, but that's the truth." Clearly,
nowhere in Europe had the human rights crusade
transcended the reliance on words.

VI.

Carter embarked on his human rights endeavor convinced that the public demanded no less. Mark L.
Schneider, deputy assistant secretary of state for
human rights and humanitarian affairs, declared in
October, 1977, that "the people of this country
want a foreign policy that is in accord with our
values. We believe that a foreign policy that
fails to reflect those values will not receive, nor
deserve, the support of the American people." Undoubtedly, Carter's humane intentions, especially
when contrasted with the attitudes of previous administrations, appealed to the deepest instincts of
the American people. Columnist Anthony Lewis of
the *New York Times* expressed the reaction of many
when he wrote: "After the dark years in which many
of us became ashamed of the things done in America's name, it simply feels good to hear a president
denounce torture and inhumanity in the most direct
way. We know there are limits to what we can do
for the victims. But we would be poor heirs to the
Declaration of Independence if we did not believe

in the eventual power of words." Perhaps it was
true, as Vance once suggested, that the message of
the American Revolution had encouraged and inspired
other nations and peoples. That, however, had
never been a matter of foreign policy.

If Americans shared the president's concern for
human rights, few understood what an effective
policy embraced or the possible cost of such basic
human needs as food, shelter, and health care. The
widespread adherence to the ideal of human better-
ment was no evidence that either Congress or the
public believed its promotion worth the cost. Most
Americans did not appear greatly troubled by the
lapse in the country's domestic performance on human rights. Abroad the challenge was great.
Amnesty International reported that serious violations of human rights continued in 119 countries.
But government costs, inflation, sagging dollars,
and soaring trade deficits had long undermined the
magnanimity of Americans toward the oppressed of
other lands. The absence of a working consensus on
human rights limited the administration to programs
that required neither cost nor risk. Not only did
the United States officially ignore the genocide of
possibly one million Cambodians, it did little for
the thousands of refugees who managed to escape.
The Carter administration acknowledged the American
obligation for the victims of the Vietnam war, for
many were in trouble with their governments because
of past association with American policies and
programs. But the care and feeding of refugees can
be expensive; within the United States, moreover,
refugees compete for scarce jobs.

The constant plea of Third World leaders for
more and more economic assistance clashed with the
American public's preference for reduced taxes and
domestic recovery. Whatever the nation's limited
concern for the plight of the poor in Asia and

65

Africa, Congress never revealed less interest in
foreign aid than it did in 1978. Congressman
Clement J. Zablocki, chairman of the House International Affairs Committee, declared that selling
foreign aid to Congress would be "about as successful as selling ice cream freezers at the North Pole
or fur-lined parkas in Africa." The United States
foreign aid program had declined to less than 1
per cent of the federal budget. In 1978 the country ranked thirteenth among seventeen donor nations
in the percentage of national income devoted to foreign development assistance. Carter's stress on
human rights would, he hoped, reflect American
values. His actual policies, reflecting national
priorities, did precisely that.

What the Carter leadership achieved for human
rights defied accurate measurement. The United
States, Washington officials agreed, could not and
would not claim credit for the gains that occurred.
But they could point to a new worldwide interest in
human rights; to the heavier price that governments
paid for their repressions; to the changing image
of the United States; and to the decisions of some
countries to release political prisoners and grant
permission to international agencies, such as the
International Red Cross and Amnesty International,
to conduct investigations within their borders. In
the administration's failure to achieve more there
is nothing strange. Whatever its power or self-
assigned obligation, no nation has ever succeeded
in serving much more than its own interests. Principles, when permitted to create objectives that
transcend the country's historic and clearly perceived interests, eliminate the possibilities of a
functioning foreign policy in like measure. Policy
goals unsupported by generally recognizable interests will not receive much credence elsewhere. The
country's power to create a utopia on either side
of the Iron Curtain was always limited; this fact

alone eliminated the nation's general obligation to humanity. Because no government, in its foreign policies, is compelled to do what it cannot do, the United States might more profitably and legitimately seek the fulfillment of its ideals at home. Human rights, wherever they exist, thrive best under conditions of international relaxation. Thus the country could have no higher purpose abroad than to maximize world stability by protecting its friends, to the extent of its capabilities, against aggressive war. It was the American contribution to victory in the two world wars of this century, it is well to remember, that gave this nation its reputation as the defender of freedom.

HUMAN RIGHTS IN SOVIET POLITICAL CULTURE

EDWARD L. KEENAN

It is most appropriate that the issue of human rights/civil rights should be raised as an aspect of American foreign policy by the most actively experiential Christian we have had in the White House in some time. Several points have been made about the very specific oddity of the Western tradition of individual rights based in Christianity and the late Roman and other Western experiences, and with the Enlightenment shaped in the form in which we know it. We might consider whether it is an ethnocentric or, how shall we say, an evangelical thrust that makes us want to extend this idea to others. It is clearly culturally defined, but so are the wheel, wine-making, and a lot of other good things. I think that a good idea deserves to be shared. But I will not discuss the many general aspects that I had intended to use as an introduction. Instead, let me turn immediately to the Russian case, which fits rather nicely between what we call "East" and "West." I think it is a useful substitution to try "traditional" and "nontraditional" or "modern" and "premodern" or something that does not have the undertone of Eurocentric terminology, but in any case it is clear that the Russian experience lies somewhere between the Chinese and our own.

I would like to examine first some of the historical developmental aspects that seem to have established the Russian tradition and then some of the importations from the West that have, to one or another extent, influenced it. I will finish with the obligatory comments about implications for American behavior.

The Russians, of course, cannot boast the millenia of Western civilization, but they too have been around for some time. And it is fortunate that we are able, with regard to the Great Russians, to capture many of the aspects of the formative centuries of Russian culture because they are so recent. I am going to discuss only the Great Russian political culture, and not that of the other East Slavs who have much in common with them, and I am not going to describe the culture of the other non-Russian populations of the Soviet Union, although I think we should keep in mind that one of the major civil rights or human rights problems in the Soviet Union is the position of the non-Russian majority.

For the purposes of the discussion of Soviet politics one can, with great confidence, equate the Great Russian political culture with "Soviet" political culture. In my view, which is not universally shared, an indelible imprint was laid upon that political culture by the circumstances of colonization in the northern part of the East European plain, a process that lasted from the earliest penetration of Slavs around 900 A.D. until the collectivization. I stress this fact because the womb of Russian political attitudes, of attitudes about self, and about society, about such things as the individual and his relationship to the group, was the world of subsistence agriculture of the Great Russian village in the forest zone roughly north of, let us say, a line drawn between Chernigov and Kazan.

This was a homeland very inhospitable, where

nature was stingy and capricious. All of the homeland of the Great Russians and the womb of their
culture lies, in terms of latitude, above the
southern tip of Hudson's Bay. Moscow is at the
latitude of Sitka. This was land that no one really
wanted until roughly the beginning of the second
millennium, when it was that a very specific kind of
Slavic agriculturalist hit the combination of social,
technological, and cultural adaptation mechanisms
that made significant agricultural colonization in
this territory possible. Over the seven or eight
hundred years of which I write, these Slavs were re-
markably successful where others had failed. They
were successful for a number of reasons, but one
can, I think, reduce these--in terms of the subject
before us--to the evolution of attitudes about man,
society, and nature that lay at the heart of later
Russian attitudes about these subjects.

The circumstances, I am sure, are familiar.
They were, particularly, favorite subjects for the
first chapter of books of Russian history thirty or
forty years ago. In recent times I think they have
been disregarded, but they are still there: very
sparsely settled, pristine forests, a growing season, or agricultural season, of maybe five months,
very poor soil, and yields that are equivalent to
the yields of Carolingian times in Western Europe.
Such conditions forced the Slavs to make what we
now call "trade-offs," the forms of cultural adaptation that set up the genetic structure of their
political culture. In this environment a single
individual, man or domestic beast, was simply not a
viable creature for very long; indeed, a single
family was probably not viable because of high
mortality, the contingent nature of agricultural
success, and for other reasons as well.

What was required in this environment was a con-
certed effort rather like that one reads about in

the anthropological literature concerning cultures
in very marginal areas, where the individual, most
kinds of activities, and most symbolic representa-
tions of these activities and relationships are
subordinated to a single goal: survival. This basic
objective lay behind the pattern of this culture--
the continuation of lines of livestock, lines of
humans (the distinctions are not nearly as great in
a culture like this as they are in our own), not
justice, not the preservation of a way of life as
the nineteenth-century populists thought, but the
preservation of life itself. For this reason the
notion that an individual had autonomous individual
existence was not only discouraged, but for good
reason it was vigilantly opposed. Of course the
limitations on individual autonomy were part of a
larger contract, which also provided that if one got
pneumonia or tuberculosis, or if his horse rolled on
him, or if his barn burned, the others would support
him and keep him alive, both as a valuable human resource in their little economy and because they knew
their turn was next. It was clear to participants
what the trade-offs were, and an individual who de-
parted from the group, or got rich and didn't share,
knew the simple sanctions he faced. I am sure that
you are all familiar with such arrangements in one
or another peasant culture. But there was one
aspect of the Russian case that has not been sufficiently explored, namely, that a very specific
view of man was imposed by this culture, as a result
of an internalization of both the image of society
and order and the pessimistic view of the prospects
for man. With regard to the order of the village as
a whole, organized social and productive life in the
village seems to have been considered to be a kind
of conspiracy against nature. With regard to more
complicated political organizations, government was
considered a kind of conspiracy against chaos.

With regard to the individual personality, it

seems that the challenging environment and the
rather demanding cycle of life were quite stressful.
For many months one did very little but try to keep
warm, do a little whittling, repair the stove, or
one thing or another, and then one was suddenly
thrust into a very dramatic spring thaw and a very
fast, balmy growing season that demanded long days
and little sleep. The demands imposed not only by
nature but by the culture were enormous and exhaust-
ing. Any member of the culture had ample experiential reason to believe that the human was quite
frail. The exertion required led, quite predictably,
to cases of "spinning off" from this cycle into
drunkenness and various forms of manic gratification
that were damaging to the village because a few lost
man-days were a threat to everyone's basic viability.

As a result of this and other things I am not
able to go into here, there developed a rather pessimistic view of human nature; I do not mean to
pose this distinction in overly stark terms, but if
we could agree that the Mediterranean view of man
and some of the traditions in the West allow a
little bit of hope for man--say, that 51 per cent
"approve" and count on man to survive and to do the
right thing--then I would say that the expectation
seems in the Russian case to have been somewhat less
optimistic--let's say 49 per cent. The implications
of this small difference are significant, and helped
lead to the development of a pessimistic notion
about the stability of society, which, of course, is
a very important underlying aspect of our own expectations about civil rights.

Such were some features of the dominant culture,
the culture in which, until our times, 90 per cent
of Great Russians lived. There were two little subcultures that developed by the fifteenth or sixteenth centuries worth mentioning because they were
politically dominant and tended to influence Russian

political institutions and Russian law. One of
these is that of the small, hereditary, clan-or-
ganized cavalry called the Russian gentry (originally aristocracy). This culture was not agricultural
and had not really had the experience of the agricultural ambiance that we have talked about. However, its organization was also, in its own way,
very efficient and demanding: Its function was to
organize social life and political and military life
in this same dismal forest, and to extract the resources for those activities from its scattered
and basically subsistence agricultural population.
The way in which this subculture, the great clans,
organized their life was rather more like Chinese
life; that is, it was an extensive clan system, with
elders who possessed the sanctions and oppressions
needed to permit them to perform their military
functions, increase wealth, spread it among all
viable sword-carrying males in the clan, and to
perform the functions so crucial to the expansion of
the Muscovite state. The people who stood at the
apex of these clans--and they were unchallenged
traditional elders--the great *boyars*, formed an
oligarchy interlocking with the one family that was
different from all the others, namely, the dynasty,
in whose current representatives they vested
despotic, primarily mythical, autocratic powers.
In fact, the oligarchs ran the system, and the
czars, in my view, counted for little. Now there
are very different cultures involved. For example,
there was only one family in all of Russia, namely,
the dynasty, that practiced primogeniture, and it
was practiced by that family because its crucial
function was not to maintain land or flocks but
biological succession. The people with whom this
family intermarried, the members of these clans,
practiced just the opposite, namely, the absolute
sharing among all males not only of clan property,
but seniority within the family, and so on. In
such clans the first son was followed by the second

74

son, and the first son of the second son, and so on, a very complicated thing. But it was clearly a corporate collateral generation ruling together. The peasants were still different, for they redistributed property and power in the village; although they had household organizations that had an elder, that is, they redistributed without strict regard for family lines.

Thus we have three different cultures operating, each of them a "traditional" society in which honor, obedience, seniority, all play highly important roles. In every one of these variations of Russian culture the notion of the autonomous was as shocking, as dangerous, as a loose cannon on deck. Now, as this clan organization and the dynasty developed a bureaucratic state, there appeared still another culture, the bureaucratic culture, which was different in its marriage arrangements and everything else from all of these, but which essentially merged with the gentry. As the nineteenth century wore on the dynasty and the gentry merged in many ways culturally, and by the late nineteenth century there were really only two cultures. But as they merged they tended to reinforce the things that they had in common and to discard the things that made them separate. The things they had in common were the restriction of individual rights for the sake of the larger group and a commitment to a broad consensual decisionmaking process involving the elders or leaders of any given corporate unit. This openness, however, had two restrictions: one was that all decisions ultimately had to be taken unanimously, that is, in the final analysis, once a decision had been made, all those in the hut, whoever they were, whether heads of families, heads of ministries, or whatever, had to accede to the decision. That was the price of their membership. A typical situation was that the one who had opposed the ultimate decision most violently would be forced to make the first speech in favor of the final decision, after it had been made. The second rule was that under no circumstances could any partisan or individual or contrary views be taken outside the complex. These were what you might call the prices willingly paid for order in a universe in which, by common agreement, stability was a miracle and governance was a conspiracy against chaos.

At the very end of the nineteenth century a part of the nonpeasant culture came under the influence of Western ways. ·Industrialization hit Great Russian culture, as it has hit others since, very hard. Change took place rapidly, bringing mobility, urbanization, and all the familiar phenomena. The transcription process of the culture, which is used to hold it together while changing, began to speed up so fast that essentially it got out of control. I would argue that in the arts, in music, in architecture, in poetry, and in the social culture of various institutions, in any number of ways, a small Westernized part of the urbanized upper classes got to the point where their culture was changing so fast they they could not socialize and interact with the rest of society or even, in a sense, with themselves, through normal socialization and culturalization processes. So a society, for example, that had always had a strong and functional commitment to secrecy began to demand freedom of the press-- and got freedom of the press in 1905, remarkable freedom of the press, freedom of the press that people could hardly handle. A society that had never had laws that really described what was going on or that anyone really believed in, began trying to write constitutions. A society in which centralization had been a crucial aspect of control because of the danger in an enormous empire of regional separatism, began suddenly to decentralize and the upper classes, and even the governing circles, began to foster the growth of local landowners' organizations, city and municipal governments, and all manner of similar things. In sum, things began to get turned inside out in the political culture in a way that is analogous to what happened in the arts in this part of the world--to academic art with Kandinsky or to conservatory music with Stravinsky, for example.

The revolution did many things to and for many people, but in the context we are interested in, I would say that probably the most significant was that, together with the first and second wars, and with the collectivization and purges, it effectively removed from society the bearers of the portion of the national culture that had been running ahead of themselves, and turned over the dominant positions in the culture and in the political arena to persons who had been acculturated within the other tradition, namely, the village peasant culture. The revolution and the industrialization and all the processes associated with them, in my view, ran their course from about 1890 until just before World War II. By the end of the purges Great Russian society had removed that cancerous growth, changed the direction of social process, and had begun to stabilize again. It is one of the striking things about Soviet culture that by almost any sociological, cultural, industrial, or political measure, Soviet society in 1939 was stable, it was resilient, and it had reknit as the conservative, risk-averse, chaos-avoiding society it is today. It is that, I think, which explains why Soviet society and the Soviet political system and political culture survived the Second World War with essentially no significant changes. The stratification, the political élite, or the ideology had its little ups and downs, but the basic fact is that anybody who had a key to the washroom in the Kremlin in 1939 still had it in 1946, and if he is still alive, has it now.

Where do human rights fit in this culture, traditionally or in the present? One of the questions that comes up is the place of Christianity in all this. What happens when Christianity in its Balkan, Slavic, Byzantine form comes to this Great Russian village? I would have to say that those elements of the message that eventually were realized in the Western tradition--in St. Paul's words, "There is neither Greek nor Jew, nor slave nor free, nor man nor woman, but we are all one in Christ"--were not, in the circumstances of the Russian village, preserved and activated in later development for a number of reasons. One reason was that the bearer of this message, to the extent that he knew it at all, the village priest, was, like the Greek priest in the Balkans, more of the village than he was of St. Paul. It was the Russian tradition that these positions were hereditary, and the village priest was essentially indistinguishable from a peasant in many respects. Moreover, it is clear, as far as we can tell, that he was subject to the same forces in the conspiracy against nature as any other member of the village. With regard to such exalted notions, one must remember the very meager development of academies or schools in Russia--until the seventeenth century there was no such thing--and the fact that just about the time the kind of levels of literacy and theological discussion and education that are characteristic of medieval Europe were established in Russia, Russia began to career into a Westernizing and developmental process that, from Peter's time, kept changing the rules. The enormous wrenching of the traditional culture that went on, particularly with regard to the Christian tradition --official support, official restriction, sociological changes of all kinds--all of these seem to have forestalled the kind of development that took place in the West.

To move to the present situation and where we

stand, I feel that one essential element in the view of human rights, namely, the view of man, has not changed much, even in our time. A major reason is that one essential element necessary to such a change, that is, a stable society, has only recently been established. Social contract involves "ninety-nine-year leases" in a sense, in a very real spiritual sense, i.e., some kind of shared confidence that commitments, reciprocal commitments, limitations, options that are chosen with one set of priorities, will be redeemable in the same stable society at a later time. The experience of recent generations of Russians--two savage wars, collectivization, the purges--has reinforced their pessimistic view of the fabric of society and the nature of man. There are still large numbers of influential individuals in the Soviet Union who have had shocking and sobering experiences that pervade their view of man and society, and one must expect that their feelings about risk-producing liberties will be different from those of citizens of more fortunate societies. On the other hand we have in the Soviet Union a case in which, in my view, there is no longer any justification, on a comparative anthropological basis, of the continuation of traditional limitations on individual autonomy, because the society has already, in fact, abandoned most of the supports that the traditional society gives an individual in return for loss of autonomy and has converted to a modern configuration for the benefit of a very few--the members of the Party.

Thus, this is a situation in which the discussion of civil and human rights in a modern and even Westernized context makes some sense, for I feel that a stable life, a stable society, and a modern configuration of social relations exist now, or are coming into existence, in the Soviet Union. It is only the selfish behavior of those who were the first to seize its fruits and levers that is holding back an

79

evolution toward more modern attitudes about man
and his individual rights.

HUMAN RIGHTS IN CHINESE POLITICAL CULTURE

SHAO-CHUAN LENG

There are two extreme approaches to human rights issues concerning Asian and other developing countries. One is to use exclusively Western standards of liberalism and democracy to measure those countries' institutions and practices. The other is to regard people in those societies as too preoccupied with the problems of survival and development to afford the "luxury" of individual rights. This paper rejects both of these approaches and subscribes instead to the following assumptions.

First, human rights are not just a Western concern but have a universal validity, with contributions from all the major civilizations.[1] An examination of the Universal Declaration of Human Rights and the International Covenants on Political and Civil Rights and on Economic, Social and Cultural Rights shows the existence of an international norm and consensus that bears influence from both Western and non-Western systems of thought. Second, the two sets of rights (political and civil rights; economic and social rights) may receive different degrees of emphasis from countries of diverse backgrounds and conditions, but they are closely interwoven and cannot be practically separated.[2] Any suggestion that a country can justifiably sacrifice one set of rights for the other is not only erroneous but also harmful. Popular demands for basic freedoms in

India, Iran, and several Latin American countries prove that people in Third World countries do care about individual rights.

The above observations provide us with a conceptual framework for analysis of human rights in traditional and contemporary China.

I. *Human Rights in the Traditional Culture*

When dealing with the question of human rights, one finds considerable ambivalence and certain contradictions in traditional Chinese political culture. The concept of "inalienable rights," for instance, was never developed in Imperial China. Nor were such ideas as constitutionalism and majority rule. As is often mentioned, the Confucian doctrine held an elitist view that expounded hierarchical social and human relationships and a paternalistic form of government. Emphasis was on the group over the individual, social stability over self-realization, duties over rights, age over youth, male over female, and mental labor over manual labor.

On the other hand there were also democratic traits in Chinese civilization. Despite the dominant role of Confucianism, intellectual freedom and religious eclecticism prevailed in the past. The toleration of other thought systems and the coexistence of different religions are a well-known fact. Taoism as a philosophy advocated naturalism and condemned government meddling. As popular religions, both Taoism and Buddhism were concerned with the fate or salvation of the individual and stood for spiritual autonomy and freedom. Even Confucianism, while stressing man's particular place in society, exalted the moral worth of the individual and the attainment of his full development through self-cultivation. From the Confucian point of view, education was an essential means to personal perfection

82

and open to everyone regardless of social background. Confucius said: "With education, there is no class distinction."[3] In this connection it should be noted that the civil service examination system, with all its flaws and distortions, did provide some degree of social mobility and equal opportunity for educated and talented men.[4]

Although Confucian teachings put an accent on individual duties in a variety of social relations, the principle of reciprocity was, however, equally emphasized with respect to rights and obligations in each human relationship. When discussing government, Confucius said that the ruler should behave like a ruler; the minister, minister; the father, father; the son, son.[5] Mencius went further to say: "When the sovereign treats his ministers as his hands and feet, they regard him as their bellies and hearts; when he treats them as his dogs and horses, they regard him as merely one of their fellows; when he treats them as grass and dirt, they regard him as a robber and an enemy."[6]

It is true that the Chinese emperor was an autocratic ruler possessed of all legislative, executive, and judicial powers. There were neither constitutional checks nor formal procedures to elect or vote out a government. Nevertheless, the imperial authority was subject to a number of restraints both in practice and in the writings of ancient sages.[7] First, the emperor, in exercising his powers, was bound by rules, traditions, and precedents established through the ages. As the head of the Confucian state, he was expected to rule virtuously and benevolently in the interest of public welfare. The ruler without virtue, in the words of Mencius, could be no ruler at all.[8] Second, the censorial institution constituted another check on the Chinese sovereign. While sometimes they were punished and even put to death by tyran-

nical rulers, the censors managed through the years
to maintain their position of independence and integrity as critics of the government. Third, the
size of the country and the laissez-faire approach
to government by the Taoists combined to curb the
power of the central authority, which had to rule
the population through local intermediaries, thus
leaving the individual considerable leeway to enjoy his life and group protection. Finally, the
most important constraint on the Chinese monarch
was the theories of the mandate of heaven and the
right of revolution. According to the classical
teachings, the emperor ruled in trust from heaven
for the well-being of the people; and when he mis-
ruled, his right to rule was automatically for-
feited. *The Book of History* says: "Heaven sees as
the people see, heaven hears as the people hear."[9]
This concept that the people were the ultimate
sovereign and that their interest should be the
paramount concern was emphatically stated by Mencius
as follows: "The people are of first importance;
the state is the next; the ruler is the least important."[10] As a corollary to the mandate of
heaven, Chinese political theory sanctioned the
people's revolts against oppressive rulers. A successful revolution was considered a justified
revolution and a clear proof of the withdrawal of
heaven's mandate from the overthrown government.
One passage from the *Book of Changes* reads: "The
revolutions led by T'ang and Wu were in accord with
the order of the heaven and in response to the wish
of the people."[11]

One of the main controversies in traditional
China was over the role of law between the Confucians, who advocated the rule of *Li* (moral code)
and the Legalists, who expounded the rule of *Fa*
(positive law). The result was the coexistence of
Li and *Fa* in Chinese society, with the latter play-
ing a secondary role. Auxiliary as law was to the

rule of Morality, the Chinese throughout their long
history promulgated many codes of importance and
breadth. Even though law was mainly designed to
protect political and social order rather than individual rights, imperial China did develop elaborate rules and procedures to curb arbitrary
official action or miscarriage of justice. Furthermore, there was a noticeable recognition of such
doctrines as equality before the law and judicial
independence. While the Confucians did favor differing treatment according to individual rank,
relationship, and specific circumstance, the Legalists forcefully asserted the principle that everyone
should be equal before the law and that law should
have no respect for personal status.[12] "The law
cannot fawn on the noble," said Han Fei Tzu, "just
as the string cannot yield to the crooked. Whatever
the law applies to, the wise cannot reject nor the
bold defy. Punishment for faults must never skip
ministers, nor rewards for good actions fail to
reach commoners."[13] Even the Confucian School, it
should be pointed out, accepted the concept of
supremacy of law and judicial independence once a
crime was committed.[14]

II. *Impact of the West*

The Western impact on Chinese society during the
modern period was best manifested in the May 4th
Movement of 1919. With "democracy and science" as
guiding concepts, the movement led by the new intelligentsia espoused sweeping changes and liberation from traditional bonds.[15] From this intellectual ferment emerged two opposite groups, the
liberal-democratic on the one hand and the Communist
on the other. The former stood for liberalism and
Western patterns of government and society. The
latter embraced Marxism-Leninism and advocated
class struggle to liberate China and the Chinese

85

masses from foreign and domestic exploitation in the name of social justice. Between the two poles there were large numbers of Chinese intellectuals who varied in the degree of their receptiveness to Western culture.

Of all Western ideas and values the most attractive to many scholars and leaders of modern China appeared to be nationalism rather than individualism. Even liberal thinkers tended to be mainly concerned with the political rather than civil component of Western liberalism. In other words, they were more interested in securing political participation in the government than in promoting civil liberties. As a matter of fact, some of them interpreted "individualism" as self-indulgence, void of public spirit and unsuitable to China's needs. Dr. Sun Yat-sen, whose Three People's Principles represented a conscientious effort to synthesize Western ideas and Chinese traditions, argued against "too much individual freedom" at the expense of "national freedom":

Why has China become a sheet of loose sand? Simply because of excessive individual liberty. ...Europeans rebelled and fought because they had too little liberty. But we, because we have had too much liberty without any unity and resisting power, because we have become a sheet of loose sand and so have been invaded by foreign imperialism,...must break down individual liberty and become pressed together into an unyielding body like the firm rock which is formed by the addition of cement to sand.[16]

The cement Sun spoke of was his Principle of Nationalism, which called for self-sacrifice and subordination of individual desires to national liberation. His Principle of Democracy provided a period of "political tutelage" in which the

Kuomintang would use the one-party rule to train the Chinese people for future constitutional government. In the Principle of People's Livelihood, Sun offered the twin policies of "equalization of land ownership" and "control of capital" to advance human welfare and prevent class conflicts.

One of the most tangible results of the Western impact on pre-1949 China was found, at least on paper, in the system of law under the Nationalist government. In the early 1930's a complete set of modern laws, known as the Six Codes (Organic Law, Commercial Law, Civil Code, Criminal Code, Civil Code of Procedure, and Criminal Code of Procedure), were enacted and promulgated by the Republic of China. Essentially of Continental type with a dash of Anglo-American influence, those codes were impressive both in concept and in draftsmanship. In 1947 the Nationalist government adopted a constitution that contained a bill of rights guaranteeing all personal liberties and rights, including equality before the law and *habeas corpus*.[17] The gap between legal niceties and political facts was considerable, however, as the ROC government's preoccupation with the Sino-Japanese War in 1937-45 and the civil war in 1945-49 rendered many of the promised freedoms and rights rather academic.

III. *Human Rights in the People's Republic of China*

The status of human rights in the People's Republic of China (PRC) is a controversial subject. Critics of the PRC tend to focus attention on Peking's violations of human rights without giving credit to some positive accomplishments in China. Equally one-sided are those who justify curbs on individual rights in the PRC on the grounds of Chinese authoritarian tradition and the imperatives of national security and economic development. In an attempt to present a more balanced picture, I will examine all pertinent facts concerning human rights in the PRC's law and practice, as well as the post-Mao leadership's promise of certain minimum guarantees of individual rights.

To begin with it should be noted that the PRC has made substantial gains in economic and social areas over the past thirty years. Granted, China is still a poor country and the standard of living of the Chinese people remains quite low. Nevertheless, the vast majority of the people have been provided with the basic essentials of food, clothing, and shelter. There is also provision free of charge or at nominal rates of medical and educational services to the bulk of the population. Despite the fluctuating record of its economic policy, the Communist government has done much to alleviate or eradicate problems of major inequalities, poverty, disease, hunger, and illiteracy in China.[18] A feeling of national pride and a sense of social consciousness and dedication to "public good" have also been instilled in the Chinese people as a whole.

On the other hand, if the Chinese people are really to enjoy the fruits of the revolution and the current "long march" to modernization, improvement must be made in the areas of political and civil rights. Official denial notwithstanding, the present leaders in Peking obviously are aware that China has a human rights problem. Their pledges of strengthening "socialist legality" and protecting basic freedoms are undoubtedly designed to restore the morale and enthusiasm of China's intellectuals, officials, and workers, whose active support is essential to the success of the modernization program. In this connection we shall first examine legal provisions in China with regard to individual rights.

A. *Human Rights in the Chinese Legal System*

Two types of law have coexisted and competed with each other in the PRC. One may be called the jural (formal) model, and the other societal (informal) model. The years 1954-57 saw the ascendency of the jural model in China, marked by the adoption of a constitution, organic legislation for the courts and procuracy, and a series of substantive and procedural laws and regulations. China's progress toward a stable legal order was brought to an abrupt end by the antirightist campaign of 1957-58, the result of which was the disruption of the codification effort and the assumption of a dominant role in law enforcement by the Party and the police at the expense of the judiciary and procuracy. The jural model suffered another serious setback during the Cultural Revolution of 1966-69, when "smashing all bourgeois legal institutions" became the slogan of the day. There is little question that Mao Tse-tung's bias against bureaucratization and preference for the mass line were responsible for the PRC's emphasis on the societal model of law over the jural model and on the politicization of the entire legal process.[19]

The 1954 Constitution of the PRC adopted at the time of China's legal experiment contained nineteen articles (Articles 85-105) on "fundamental rights and duties of citizens." Among the basic rights guaranteed were freedom of speech, press, assembly, association, and demonstration, inviolability of the person and inviolability of the home. In the 1975 constitution, which showed a strong Maoist influence, the provisions for individual rights were reduced to four articles (Articles 26-29). While the basic freedoms mentioned above were retained with qualifications, a number of individual rights previously guaranteed were conspicuously missing, including freedom of residence, freedom to

89

change residence, right to rest, right to counsel, and freedom to engage in scientific research and cultural activities. To its short list of promised freedoms the 1975 document did add such new features as the right to strike (Article 28) and right to speak out freely and write big character posters (Article 13). The post-Mao leadership's sensitivity to the need of legality is reflected in the new constitution of 1978, which bears a close resemblance to the 1954 constitution and restores to the people many rights dropped since then. Of the sixteen articles on citizens' rights and duties (Articles 44-59) in the 1978 constitution, fourteen essentially revive the provisions in the 1954 document. A couple of new items from the 1975 constitution are also incorporated in the present constitution, e.g., the right to strike, the right to write posters (Article 45), and the duty to support the leadership of the Communist Party of China (Article 56).[20]

A similar development has occurred in the judicial field. In 1954 the constitution (Articles 73-84) and relevant organic laws established the regular structure of the people's court and the people's procuracy (the supervisor of the legality of the actions of state organs, state personnel, and citizens). Equality before the law, the right of legal defense, the right to an open trial, protection against arbitrary arrest, and independence of the judiciary were guaranteed by the constitution and other documents. All such guarantees, however, were eliminated by the 1975 constitution, which reduced the provisions for the judicial system from twelve articles to just one (Article 25). To conform to the prevailing practice, it required the application of the mass line to trials and transferred the powers and functions of the procuratorial organs to the police. In an attempt to strengthen the legal system, the 1978 constitution revives the rights of the accused to defense and to an open trial and the participation of people's accessors in the administration of justice (Article 41). It also reinstitutes the procuracy and reestablishes the requirement for the police to have the approval of the judiciary or the procuracy before making an arrest (Articles 43 and 47). While failing to restore provisions on equality before the law and the independence of the courts, the new constitution does deemphasize the mass line in trying cases and makes the local courts accountable again to the local people's congresses (Article 42) instead of to both the local people's congresses and their executive organs as required by the 1975 constitution.

B. *Restrictions and Abuses*

In the campaign against the "gang of four," the current leadership has attacked Mao's widow and her associates for creating a state of lawlessness, arbitrary rule, and "Fascist tyranny" during the years 1966-76. The disgraced radicals have been accused of subjecting political opponents to arbitrary arrest, extended detention, and endless struggle meetings. Tens of thousands of innocent people are said to have been cruelly tortured and prosecuted by the followers of the "gang of four."[21]

Whether or not it is fair to blame the "gang of four" alone for past abuses, these charges actually amount to an official acknowledgment of the existence of human rights restrictions and violations in the PRC. One obvious restriction is the unlimited power the Party exercises over all state organs and human activities. Personal mobility and occupational choice are rigidly limited through the Party's control of ration coupons and travel permits.[22] The 1978 constitution has not restored the people's right to choose their residence, apparently because of Peking's intention to continue the rustication policy that has sent millions of middle-school graduates to the countryside to work since the late 1960's.[23]

Another major inhibition to individual freedom in China has been the people's fear of deviating from the official line lest they be labeled "class enemies," bearing the brunt of the repressive measures of the "dictatorship of the proletariat." Article 18 of the new constitution provides for the deprivation of rights of the following categories of persons: "landlords," "rich peasants," "reactionary capitalists," "counterrevolutionaries," "bad elements," and "newborn bourgeois elements."

In the administration of justice, the police and party committees have been given too much discretional power unchecked by any outside institutional restraint. Without published codes the people are uncertain what is forbidden and what rights they can really exercise. Some offenses may receive entirely different judgment, depending upon such factors as timing, place, class background, etc. There is no privilege against self-recrimination and self-accusation under the party policy of "leniency to those who confess and severe punishments to those who resist."[24]

The concern for the PRC's political repression has prompted the recent publication by Amnesty International of a 176-page report on political imprisonment in China. The report noted that during the past thirty years large numbers of Chinese have been subjected to extreme social and mental pressures, imprisonment, and even execution purely for political reasons. A number of practices were singled out as flagrant violations of human rights. Among them are the following:
Deprivation of political and civil rights on the

basis of the individual's "class origin" or political background.
Employment of periodical "mass mobilization campaigns" to identify and purge people dissenting from official policy.
Imposition of "informal" or "administrative" sanctions on political offenders without judicial investigation or other legal process.
Detention of political offenders for a long period before trial and lack of formal guarantees of their right to defense.
Use of trial as merely formal meetings to announce the sentence.

The report praised the current Chinese leadership for certain steps taken to redress past abuses, including a decision adopted in the spring of 1978 on the release of, or restoration of rights to, thousands of people who had been classified as "rightists" since 1957. However, Amnesty International was concerned by the continuation in China of arrests and executions on political grounds (now against alleged supporters of the "gang of four") and the presence of provisions in the new constitution and other legal documents violating individual rights and permitting repressive measures against political offenders. It therefore appealed to Peking to take steps "toward signing and ratifying the United Nations International Covenant on Civil and Political Rights, to guarantee to its citizens their fundamental human rights and to safeguard these rights by appropriate judicial procedures."25

C. *Recent Political Ferment and Liberalization Moves*

One of the adverse effects of the PRC's past repression of political dissent has been the serious damage done to the morale of the intelligentsia, whose talent and innovation are badly needed to achieve Peking's ambitious goals of modernization.[26] During the 1950's the non-Communist intellectuals who strongly criticized the Party's bureaucratic practices and its repression of any potential opposition in the Hundred Flowers Movement were branded and punished as "rightists" by the regime's antirightist campaign. In the 1960's those party intellectuals and bureaucrats who challenged Mao's policies and leadership became the targets of purge in the Cultural Revolution. During the 1970's, when Peking was under the influence of the "gang of four," there were two dramatic instances of political protests forcefully suppressed by the authorities. One was the Tien An Men Square riot of April 5, 1976, protesting premature removal of wreaths honoring the late Premier Chou En-lai. The radical-controlled politburo labeled the riot "counterrevolutionary," had the rioters arrested and jailed, and purged Vice-Premier Teng Hsiao-ping for alleged involvement with the incident. The other stunning demonstration of dissent was the famous Li I-che poster, entitled "On Socialist Democracy and the Legal System," which appeared on the wall of a downtown street in Canton in November, 1964. Written by three former Red guards, this 20,000-word poster accused China's political system of producing a "new clique of nobility" who "suppressed the popular masses" rising up to oppose their special privileges. It urged Peking to reestablish the rule of law and enforce such constitutional rights as freedom of speech, freedom of press, freedom of association, and freedom to air opinions in big-character posters. Branded as "class enemies," the authors were seized, "struggled against," and sentenced to imprisonment.[27]

As part of its liberalization program the current leadership in China has moved to rectify some of its predecessor's repressive measures against political dissenters. Large numbers of purged

94

"rightists," for instance, have been released and rehabilitated.[28] The verdict concerning the Tien An Men Square incident has been reversed, and the rioters are now hailed "revolutionary heroes."[29] The authors of the Li I-che poster have also been set free recently.[30]

Probably the most striking phenomenon in post-Mao China is the authorities' new toleration of public airing of complaints. There have been in recent months wall posters and street demonstrations in Peking, Shanghai, Tientsin, Wuhan, and Canton with unprecedented demands for more democracy, less dictatorship, and better living conditions. Some posters have criticized human rights violations in China and appealed to President Carter to raise the issue with the Chinese government.[31] Others have called for greater freedom of expression, the right to elect officials, and the right to publish private newspapers.[32] Still others have demanded better housing, higher pay, more consumer goods, and more foreign movies and books, including pornography.[33] Hundreds of ragged peasants from all parts of China have marched in Peking to demand food and human rights and to complain of hunger, low incomes, and the oppression of local officials.[34] Disgruntled urban yough, assigned to rural work, have rioted in Shanghai and staged a strike in Yunnan to protest "intolerable" working conditions on state farms and seek reassignment to big cities with better educational opportunities, entertainment, and food supplies.[35]

There are, of course, definite limits to which Peking will permit public display of dissent. Its current cautious toleration of free debates, nevertheless, underscores the need to win back popular confidence and build a favorable image in an all-out effort to make China a modern industrial state by the end of the century. It is for the same reason that the Chinese leaders have taken steps to revive "socialist legality." In addition to constitutional reforms, new laws and regulations have been promised to protect individual rights and to further economic development and foreign trade. Among the codes and regulations being drafted or revised are: (1) a criminal code, a code of criminal procedure, and a civil code; (2) economic regulations concerning communes, factories, labor, finance, and arbitration organs for settling economic disputes; (3) rules and regulations used in international intercourse such as those relating to the sea, contract, patents, and trademarks.[36]

In a communiqué adopted on December 22, 1978, the Central Committee of the Chinese Communist Party emphasized the need to strengthen the legal system and made a qualified commitment to "judicial independence" and "equality before the law," the two concepts contained in the 1954 constitution but unrestored in the present constitution. The pertinent section of the communiqué reads as follows:

In order to safeguard people's democracy, it is imperative to strengthen the socialist legal system so that democracy is systematized and written into law in such a way as to insure the stability, continuity and full authority of this democratic system and these laws: There must be laws for people to follow, these laws must be observed, their enforcement must be strict and lawbreakers must be dealt with. From now on, legislative work should have an important place on the agenda of the national people's congress and its standing committee. Procuratorial and judicial organizations must maintain their independence as is appropriate; they must faithfully abide by the laws, rules and regulations, serve the people's interests, keep to the facts, guarantee the equality of all people before the people's laws and deny anyone the privilege of being above the law.[37]

The encouraging statement that no one is above the law obviously does not apply to the Party, for Professor Shen Chung-ling of Peking University has stated that "the law is the embodiment of the Party's policy."[38]

Another major liberalization move made by the current leadership is the restoration of political and civil rights to the social groups that have been labeled as the "enemies of the people" for thirty years: "landlords, rich peasants, counterrevolutionaries, and bad elements." In its latest act Peking has ordered the end of discrimination against members of former "class enemies" and their descendants on "school enrollment, job allocation, joining the army, the Communist Yough League and the Party" as long as they support socialism. Not surprisingly, an important condition attached to the new policy is the individual's proper political stand--support of the party line.[39]

By the same token, the Chinese government has directed special appeals to Chinese intellectuals. Referring to the intellectuals as "members of the working class," a recent *People's Daily* article stated that people with specialist knowledge "must really have position, authority, and responsibility." In turn, it said, the intellectuals "should dedicate all their wisdom and wit to the magnificent cause of socialism and continue to work hard to speed up the realization of four modernizations."[40]

IV. *The PRC's Stand on the International Issue of Human Rights*

Peking's position on the global issue of human rights is quite complex and should be examined, first of all, in relation to its approach to international law. As shown in some special studies, the PRC is not so different from other major powers in using international law as an instrument to manage interstate relations and to advance national interest.[41] Its attitude is a selective and pragmatic one, accepting certain established norms when convenient, while rejecting or modifying others when necessary. The Chinese have strongly objected, for example, to any U.N. discussion of violations of human rights in Tibet as an interference in China's domestic affairs. At the same time, they have supported without any feeling of inconsistency U.N. resolutions against South Africa for its policy of apartheid.

Moreover, the apparent awareness of the gap between international standards on human rights and its own record has put the PRC on the defensive. Sensitive to foreign criticism, the Chinese have tended in the past to deny or minimize the existence of human rights problems in China. They have also dismissed the "human rights flap" as "nothing more than a hypocritical farce" staged by the two superpowers to throw mud at each other.[42]

All this explains China's rather puzzling behavior patterns in the U.N. with regard to human rights. The PRC has thus far declined to participate in the work of the U.N. Commission on Human Rights, although it is represented in the commission's parent body, the Economic and Social Council, as well as in the Commission on the Status of Women, another subgroup of the ECOSOC. Peking has not endorsed or signed the Universal Declaration of Human Rights, the two related International Covenants, and other U.N. multilateral treaties on human rights. It has voted favorably for a General Assembly resolution concerning respect for human rights in armed conflict, and also for Assembly resolutions condemning

the use of torture by governments. Yet Chinese
delegates have generally elected not to vote,
through abstention or nonparticipation in the voting, for many other Assembly resolutions on human
rights, including those on Chile.[43]

The major area of human rights that the PRC has
put special emphasis on is what it calls "just
struggles" against racial and colonial oppression.
Chinese spokesmen have articulated the linkage between the promotion of human rights in the world
and the elimination of racism, imperialism, colonialism, and hegemonism.[44] For this reason the
PRC has consistently taken a strong stand in supporting and advocating U.N. condemnation or sanctions against the racist regimes of southern
Rhodesia and South Africa. As part of its anti-
hegemonism device, Peking has also attacked the
USSR for serious human rights violations. For one
thing, the Soviet government is accused of imposing
a "fascist dictatorship" upon the Russian people
and of confining political dissidents in torturous
"psychiatric hospitals."[45] For another, Moscow's
"ruling clique" is indicted for enforcing the
"Russianization policy" to ruthlessly exploit and
oppress minority nationalities.[46]

On the whole, the Chinese approach to human
rights on the international scene has been highly
selective and often ambiguous. When dealing with
human rights issues in sensitive areas, where
Peking's foreign policy may suffer or its domestic
record may be vulnerable, the PRC has frequently
adopted an evasive or noncooperative stand. However, there are prospects for a change. If the
PRC's current policies of liberalization and closer
ties with the West continue, it may well become
more disposed toward participation in U.N. resolutions or international conventions on human
rights.

Conclusion

The political ferment in China today illustrates the existence of a universal yearning for human rights and the fallacy of the proposition that a society can trade off individual rights for economic development with impunity. To be sure, Chinese poster writers and street demonstrators are not pressing for the right to select their government. But they do demand the rule of law, guarantees of constitutional freedoms, and protection of fundamental rights against arbitrary official action. In this regard the Chinese can draw inspiration not only from outside sources but also from their own political culture. Despite its authoritarian tradition, some measure of intellectual freedom and personal autonomy existed in Old China. There were restraints both in theory and in practice on the power of the emperor. Moral codes and legal rules also operated to curb bureaucratic oppression of individuals.

It would be naive to interpret China's current liberalization policy as a move toward Western-style democracy. The PRC, after all, is still a Communist state. Thus, newly granted freedoms must be exercised within the boundaries of the socialist order. Enjoyment of individual rights has to be conditioned by the duty to support the Chinese Communist Party. In a recent warning to urban youths abandoning assigned farm jobs the *People's Daily* said that anyone who used the pretext of democracy to create disorder and chaos would be severely punished.[47]

Nevertheless, the steps taken by the post-Mao leadership to ease restrictions on individual rights, revitalize the legal system, and encourage limited free demonstrations are a significant beginning of a hopeful new direction for China.

They certainly constitute an "emancipation" from the Maoist straitjacket and may generate a momentum of their own. There is a good possibility that the PRC's desire to win popular support and secure foreign technology in its determined march to modernization may make the present government more responsive to increasing domestic and external pressures for expansion of human rights guarantees.

The question here is what, if anything, the United States should do about human rights in China. Those observers who think that the United States should express its concern point out rightfully that for the sake of American moral integrity and policy consistency Washington cannot just ignore the same basic human needs and desires that the Chinese people share with the rest of humanity.[48] Given Peking's sensitivity to its international image and to outside interference in its domestic affairs, this country, however, should handle the issue with tact and candidness. The Chinese ought to be praised for achievements in certain areas of human rights but criticized for deficiencies in others; their current liberalization policy should be commended and its continuity and further development encouraged. In the long run it is the expansion of Sino-American political, economic, and cultural ties and increased exchanges of persons and ideas between the two countries that are likely to have a lasting, positive impact on the advancement of human rights in China. Limited as our influence may be on China, we have every reason to do our best to help facilitate a trend there toward a better life and greater freedom for a quarter of the human race.

Notes

1. See, for example, Peter L. Berger, "Are Human Rights Universal?" *Commentary*, September, 1977, pp. 60-64; Raul S. Manglapus, "Human Rights Are Not a Western Discovery," *Worldview*, October, 1978, pp. 4-6.

2. The inseparability of the two sets of rights was the view held by a discussion group on human rights chaired by Professor Louis Sohn at an Airlie House conference in October, 1977. "Human Rights and U.S. Policy," the Stanley Foundation, *The Eighteenth Strategy for Peace Conference Report*, 13-16 October 1977, pp. 14-16. Consult also "Two Concepts of Liberty," Isaiah Berlin, *Four Essays on Liberty* (London: Oxford University Press, 1969), pp. 118-72.

3. *The Analectics*, Book 15, ch. 38.

4. The civil service examination system has been a subject of controversy. Critics have contended that the system actually worked in favor of the members of the ruling class. Chung-li Chang, *The Chinese Gentry* (Seattle: University of Washington Press, 1955), pp. 182-87; Karl A. Wittfogel, *New Light in Chinese History* (New York: Institute of Pacific Relations, 1938), pp. 11-12. Other scholars, however, have used impressive data to show that the system served to recruit into government service a significant proportion of new blood. Ping-ti Ho, *The Ladder of Success in Imperial China, 1368-1911* (New York: Columbia University Press, 1962), pp. 107-28; Edward A. Kracke, Jr., "Religion, Family, and Individual in the Chinese Examination System," in *Chinese Thought and Institutions*, ed. John K. Fairbank (Chicago: University of Chicago Press, 1957), pp. 251-68.

5. *The Analectics*, Book 12, ch. 11.

6. *Mencius*, Book 4, pt. 2, ch. 3.

7. For detailed discussion of restraints on the Chinese emperor see Shao-chuan Leng, "Chinese Law," in *Sovereignty Within the Law*, ed. Arthur Larson (Dobbs Ferry, N.Y.: Oceana Publications, 1965), pp. 245-46; Franklin W. Houn, *Chinese Political Traditions* (Washington, D.C.: Public Affairs Press, 1965), ch. 3.

8. *Mencius*, Book 1, pt. 1, ch. 8.

9. "The Great Declaration," 2. The theory of the "mandate of heaven" was developed by the Confucians from the *Book of History*.

10. *Mencius*, Book 7, pt. 2, ch. 14.

11. Ko (revolution), Tien-ti.

12. For a good analysis of the Confucian and Legalist views see Derk Bodde, "Basic Concepts of Chinese Law: The Genesis and Evolution of Legal Thought in Traditional China," *Proceedings of the American Philosophical Society*, October, 1963, pp. 382-91.

13. *Han Fei Yze*, ch. 6.

14. This is best illustrated by the dialogue between Mencius and one of his disciples over a hypothetical murder case involving the father of Emperor Shun. Leng, "Chinese Law," p. 244.

15. On this movement see Chow Tse-tsung, *The May Fourth Movement: Intellectual Revolution in Modern China* (Cambridge, Mass.: Harvard University Press, 1960).

16. Sun Yat-sen, *San Min Chu I*, trans. Frank W. Price (Shanghai: The Commercial Press, 1930), p. 210.

17. Chapter II. The text of the constitution is in *China Yearbook, 1957-58* (Taipei: China Publishing Co., 1958), pp. 687-710.

18. For a general discussion of the PRC's economic development see Alexander Eckstein, *China's Economic Revolution* (Cambridge: Cambridge University Press,

1977), and Jan S. Prybyla, *The Chinese Economy* (Columbia, S.C.: University of South Carolina Press, 1978).

19. See Shao-chuan Leng, "The Role of Law in the People's Republic of China As Reflecting Mao Tsetung's Influence," *Journal of Criminal Law and Criminology*, 68, 3 (1979): 356-73; also Jerome A. Cohen, "Reflections on the Criminal Process in China," ibid.: 323-55.

20. English texts of the three constitutions are available in, respectively, *Constitution of the People's Republic of China* (Peking: Foreign Language Press, 1954), *Document of the First Session of the Fourth National People's Congress of the People's Republic of China* (Peking: Foreign Language Press, 1975), pp. 5-9, and "The Constitution of the People's Republic of China," *Peking Review*, 17 March 1978, pp. 5-14.

21. See, for instance, *Washington Post*, 1 December 1977, p. A 34; *New York Times*, 1 March 1978, p. 1; *New York Times*, 6 June 1978, p. 1.

22. Peking's various forms of social control were described in the series of five articles by Ross Munro that appeared in the *Washington Post*, 9-13 October 1977. See also his article "China's Rigid Control," *Washington Post*, 27 November 1977, pp. C 1, C 5.

23. For a discussion of this forceful transfer of urban youth to rural areas see Thomas P. Bernstein, *Up to the Mountains and Down to the Villages* (New Haven: Yale University Press, 1977).

24. For a thorough analysis of the administration of justice in China see Cohen, *supra* note 19, pp. 331-41, and his book *Criminal Process in the People's Republic of China, 1949-1963* (Cambridge, Mass.: Harvard University Press, 1968). See also Shao-chuan Leng, *Justice in Communist China: A Survey of*

the Judicial System of the Chinese People's Republic
(Dobbs Ferry, N.Y.: Oceana Publications, 1967).

25. *Political Imprisonment in the People's Republic of China* (London: Amnesty International Publications, 1978).

26. For Peking's treatment of the intellectuals in the various political campaigns see Roderick Mac-Farquhar, *The Hundred Flowers Campaign and the Chinese Intellectuals* (New York: Praeger, 1960); Merle Goldman, *Literary Dissent in Communist China* (Cambridge, Mass.: Harvard University Press, 1967); Peter R. Moody, Jr., *Opposition and Dissent in Contemporary China* (Stanford: Hoover Institution, 1977). For a critical narrative of life in China during the Cultural Revolution and the early 1970's see Chen Jo-hsi, *The Execution of Mayor Yin* (Bloomington, Ind.: Indiana University Press, 1978), and Simon Leys, *Chinese Shadows* (New York: Viking Press, 1977).

27. Li I-che was a pen name for three young authors: Li Cheng-t'ien, Chen I-yang, and Wang Hsi-che. For the analysis and translation of the poster see Anita Chan and Jonathan Unger, eds., "The Case of Li I-che," *Chinese Law and Government*, Fall, 1977, pp. 1-112.

28. *New York Times*, 6 June 1978, p. 1; *New China News Agency* (NCNA), 16 November 1978.

29. "Heroes of Tien An Men Square," *Peking Review*, 17 November 1978, pp. 13-15; "The Truth About the Tien An Men Incident," *Jen-min jih-pao* (JMJP--*People's Daily*), 21-22 November 1978.

30. *Washington Post*, 19 January 1979, p. A 18; *NCNA*, 8 February 1979.

31. *Washington Post*, 12 December 1978, pp. A 1, A 17.

32. *Washington Post*, 26 November 1978, pp. A 1, A 29; 1 December 1978, p. A 26; 8 February 1979, p. A 17.

33. Fox Butterfield, "Freer Expression Typifies a New Dynamism in China," *New York Times*, 14 January 1979, pp. 1, 12; "The New China: Special Report," *Newsweek*, 5 February 1979, pp. 38-40.

34. *Washington Post*, 11 January 1979, pp. A 1, 11; 15 January 1979, p. A 18.

35. *Washington Post*, 12 December 1978, p. A 12; 10 February 1979, p. A 16.

36. "Discussion on Strengthening China's Legal System," *Peking Review*, 10 November 1978, pp. 5-6; "China's Socialist Legal System," 12 January 1979, pp. 29-30, and "Active Judicial Circles," p. 35.

37. "Communique of the Third Plenary Session of the 11th Central Committee of the Communist Party of China," *Peking Review*, 29 December 1978, p. 14.

38. Jay Mathews, "China Moves Gradually Toward Liberalized Legal System," *Washington Post*, 19 January 1979, p. A 18.

39. *New York Times*, 30 January, 1979, p. A 8; *Washington Post*, 8 February 1979, p. A 16.

40. "Comprehensively and Accurately Understand the Party's Policy Towards Intellectuals," *JMJP*, 4 January 1979.

41. See Jerome A. Cohen and Hungdah Chiu, *People's China and International Law* (Princeton: Princeton University Press, 1974); James C. Hsiung, *Law and Policy in China's Foreign Relations* (New York: Columbia University Press, 1972); Shao-chuan Leng and Hungdah Chiu, eds., *Law in Chinese Foreign Policy* (Dobbs Ferry, N.Y.: Oceana Publications, 1972).

42. "Absurd Champion of 'Human Rights,'" *Peking Review*, 11 March 1977, p. 23.

43. For more detailed discussion see Cohen, "Reflections on the Criminal Process in China": 252-54;

Samuel S. Kim, "China and World Order," *Alternatives*, May, 1978, pp. 567-68.

44. See, for instance, the Chinese representative's statement during the 1976 debate on Chile in the Third Committee of the General Assembly. U.N. Doc. A/C. 3/31/SR. 58 (23 November 1976), p. 7.

45. "Soviet 'Psychiatric Hospitals'--Prisons in Disguise," *Peking Review*, 11 March 1977, pp. 20-22.

46. "New Tsars Push a National Annexation Policy," *Peking Review*, 4 March 1977, pp. 20-21, "Exploitation and Oppression of Non-Russian People in Central Asia," pp. 21-23; "Crimean Tartars Demand National Equality," 22 September 1978, p. 29.

47. *JMJP*, 13 February 1979.

48. *Sino-American Relations: A New Turn*, report to the Committee on Foreign Relations, U.S. Senate, by Senator John Glenn, January, 1979 (Washington, D.C.: U.S. Government Printing Office, 1979), p.53; Jerome A. Cohen, "Human Rights in China: U.S. Should Press Issue, But Not As Barrier to Ties," *Washington Post*, 23 April 1978, p. D 2; Susan L. Shirk, "Human Rights: How About China?" *Foreign Policy*, 29 (Winter, 1977-78): 123-28.

HUMAN RIGHTS IN INDIAN POLITICAL CULTURE

RALPH BUULTJENS

Human rights, as both rhetoric and policy, has become so fashionable in recent years that a casual
observer may sometimes assume that it was an inven-
tion of the Carter administration. However, looking
at this issue from the perspective of political
traditions and cultures reminds us that questions of
human rights have engaged thoughtful participants
in many societies, in many parts of the world, for
many centuries. This focus also suggests that the
attitudes and values of nations are as much conditioned by history as by modern political theory or
ideology. India, with its heritage of an enduring
civilization, is one of the more significant examples of how current political issues, including
human rights, are inseparable from cultural themes
and continuities.

There are three preliminary observations that
outline and also limit the context of my discussion
of human rights in Indian political culture:

1. In referring to Western perceptions of human
rights, I draw on Norman Graebner's definition: The
natural rights of all persons to governments of
their own consent, to equality before the law, to
protection from governmental assault on the integrity of the person, to individual conscience, to
the right to earn a decent living, and to equality

in terms of human dignity.

2. My comments will center on the Hindu political tradition. India has produced several other socio-political cultures and traditions (including Buddist and Sikh) and has significant and influential minority groups (including Moslems and Christians). Yet, the sustaining elements and primary inheritances of Indian society have been based largely on Hindu patterns of thought and ways of life.

3. Within the Hindu tradition, which has evolved over 3,500 years, there is wide diversity of practice and faith clustered around a few central and essential themes. In discussing this tradition, my comments will necessarily be general rather than addressed to the particularities of segments of Hinduism.

India remains a very traditional society. It is the only major nation that has not had either a political or economic revolution at some time in the past three centuries. In this traditional environment, attitudes and values, concepts and goals are primarily shaped by two principal forces: religion and mythology. In the Indian context this essentially means Hinduism and the mythological models of Indian society--the heroes and heroines who incarnate patterns that become the ideals and influence the aspirations of society. It is through these two windows that I will examine Indian political culture and human rights. To that end, I will concentrate on four areas:

I. The historical and philosophic roots of human rights in Hinduism, i.e., a Hindu view of human rights.
II. The development of Hinduism and the development of dominant hero-heroine models in Indian

society, and the implication of these developments
for human rights.

III. The impact of Western influences on Hindu
political culture in the colonial period and after,
i.e., in approximately the past three centuries.

IV. The consequences of these evolutions, im-
pacts, and developments on political culture today.

I. *Historical/Philosophical Roots--Human Rights*
in Hinduism

Hinduism came to the Indian region around 3,500
years ago, at the time of the Aryan migrations in
the Vedic Ages. In both origin and development it
is essentially a congery of many different forms of
faith revolving around a few basic concepts. These
common fundamentals, beliefs shared by most Hindus,
form the core of Hinduism and are the starting
point for any discussion of human rights in Indian
political culture. For our purposes two of these
basic elements are significant and require examination.

The first theme concerns *order in the universe*.
Hinduism established both a cosmic order and a social order. Considerable individualism and metaphysical tolerance characterized the pursuit of
spiritual advancement in the cosmic order. Conformism and social rigidity became characteristic of
the social order. Originally, society was structured around economic functions and into groups
that performed those functions. These groups
gradually crystallized into a more inflexibly defined caste system. Between about 200 B.C. and
200 A.D., when the great source book of caste
definition and duty (the Laws of Manu or Manu
Smriti) was compiled, society was already effectively organized along caste lines. Although there
have been significant changes since that time, the
main grid of the caste order has continued to our day.

111

The caste system produced group solidarity and collective group obligations, an interdependence between groups, and a sense of deference to authority. The essential feature of caste was the assumption that there are fundamental and unchangeable differences in both the status and nature of human beings. These differences make it necessary for people to be governed by different norms of behavior appropriate to their station in life. A uniform standard cannot be made applicable to all men. Each group has its traditionally defined and religiously sanctioned dharma, or duty. The Bhagavad Gita, one of the most important Hindu scriptures, declares the supreme merit of performing the duty of each person's caste: "Better to do your own duty badly than another's duty well." The Laws of Manu proclaim that "obedience to caste rules is the very essence of dharma." These early sacred texts maintained that perfection could only be attained by those who fulfilled their caste obligations with dedication. Caste divisions, embracing the concept that different groups of people had different values, were the framework of society, and penalties for violation of caste functions were widely accepted.

The second relevant theme of Hinduism concerns *the Hindu perception of truth*. There are many levels of spiritual truth, although all truth is ultimately one and the same. Hindu thought rejects the concept that each individual can have the same vision of reality and that there is a single perception of truth common to all. This contrasts directly with the Christian, Islamic, and Buddhist views that all believers can share in the same vision. From the Hindu perception comes this implication: If there are many levels of truth and all are valid, there are many levels of rights and all are valid. Progressions of birth and rebirth, with different rights attached to each step, enable access to different gradations of rights. The universal application of a common set of rights for all people in a given society, at the same time, is not part of this cosmology. In addition, rights bring obligations, and the failure to perform obligations can reduce or deprive an individual of his or her rights--a theme that is antithetical to the Western view of the unalienable and inherent rights of each person.

II. *Hindu Development, Models, and Human Rights*

While these early concepts have formed an enduring framework, they were conditioned by the development of Hinduism in four areas:

1. Metaphysical tolerance led to spiritual individualism. New modes and methods of seeking salvation brought a greater degree of spiritual freedom to Hinduism.

2. Social conformism remained inflexible, although attempts to reform and change these rigidities were frequent and persistent. Some of these attempts were absorbed into the mainstream of Hindu society, others coexisted on its fringes. However, in general, the patterns of Hindu orthodoxy (including the more traditional, multidimensional views of human rights) prevailed for most of society.

3. Political thought in Hindu society was significantly influenced by the Artha-sastra (Treatise on Material Gain--an exposition of the principles of politics attributed to Kautilya, chief minister to King Chandragupta Maurya about 300 B.C.). One of the themes of this work is a pragmatic and cynical view of the purposes of government. In its reinforcement of the caste system and general approach to political order, the Artha-sastra has little use for any concept of human rights as de-

fined by Western criteria today.

4. A series of foreign conquests of Hindu areas
imposed political captivity on the internal religious base. Adjustment to this captivity and its
non-Hindu norms became necessary and resulted in
some modifications of Hindu social practices. Hindu
society learned to protect its tradition by accommo-
dation--external adjustment to the requirements of
the conqueror, internal retention of tradition, beliefs, and ways of life. Often, successful conceal-
ment enabled the tradition to survive, and occasionally the tradition provided the springboard for
Hindu nationalist revivals. Maintenance of
tradition also created an effective barrier to new
concepts of socio-political behavior--an elaborate
material and psychological resistance mechanism
against cultural intrusion.

From the historical grew the mythological. The
importance of myth is evident throughout India.
Every villager, the most illiterate peasant, is
conscious of the epics of the past and can repeat
folklore about great legendary figures, the heroes
and heroines with whom the Hindu identifies. Many
of these dynamic characters had tried to change
Hinduism and several of them succeeded. However,
while the zeal of some reformers produced results,
their efforts were not generally directed toward
introduction of Western-style human rights programs.
There are several such personality models whose
lives, as recounted from generation to generation,
have shaped the actions and the behavior of lesser
mortals in different regions of India. In recent
times four epic figures have had a special appeal
for young men--the mythological aura that extends
as a molding influence.

Krishna, an incarnation of the God Vishnu, was
possibly a great warrior of antiquity; a man who be-

came a god. His human exploits encapsulated a range of experiences, his divinity evokes extraordinary faith. Yet, neither as god nor man does Krishna related to any special image of Western-style human rights.

Chaitanya (1485-1533), a vigorous and mystical Hindu revivalist in Bengal, is often perceived as a god become a man--an incarnation of Krishna. A proponent of the Hindu school of Vaishnavism, Chaitanya was a scholar-activist who reportedly rejected much of the caste system. In that sense he was a major reformer, but his legacy is oriented more toward piety and mysticism (partly because of the mystical nature of his disappearance at the height of his fame) than toward Western concepts of human rights.

Subas Chandra Bose (1897-1945) was considered, by many of his followers, to be an incarnation of Chaitanya. Bose, a charismatic Bengali nationalist, projected himself as a warrior-ascetic. A devout Hindu, he saw some merit in both fascism and Marxism and apparently sought to fuse them with Hinduism. Bose stressed obedience, order, and discipline in his anti-British efforts: "Give me your blood and I will give you freedom." This vision of freedom was essentially anticolonial rather than socio-political. Eventually, Bose supported the Axis forces in World War II and died in a mysterious air crash while flying to Japan in August, 1945.

Mahatma Gandhi (1869-1948) combined moral traditionalism with social reform. Particularly opposed to the inequities of the caste system and the subjugation of women, Gandhi was socially compassionate and personally intolerant, demanding unchallenging obedience from his supporters. In his view, obligations and duties were as important as rights.

Profoundly dedicated to spiritual freedom and political independence, Gandhi's perception of human rights comes relatively near the Western view. Yet, there were many dogmatic restrictions (including prohibition of alcohol, vegetarianism, sexual abstinence) that he sought to impose on society and on the individual. His assassination by Hindu extremists was the price he paid for encouraging spiritual tolerance.

None of these male heroes was fully committed to the Western view of human rights. They and others of their type were creations of Hindu society. Shaped by it, they sought to reshape it, but not in Western patterns of development. The Western concept of human rights has been advocated by relatively few leaders of myth-figure stature in Indian history. Two such recent advocates have been Rabindranath Tagore and Jawaharlal Nehru. However, neither Tagore nor Nehru evokes the passionate fervor that attaches to Krishna-Chaitanya-Bose-Gandhi and projects them as exemplars.

Among women there are two dominant model types. They reflect a tension between two conceptions of woman that are present in most religious and social heritages--woman the compassionate vs. woman the power-seeker. One tradition is represented by the exemplars of the classics: Sita, the virtuous heroine of the Ramayana (written c. 300 B.C.); and Savitri, the devoted and sacrificing wife of the Mahabharata (c. 400 B.C.). These women were willing to endure great hardship for and from their husbands, voluntarily submissive and uncomplainingly loyal. Today, at most Hindu weddings, the bride's blessing is "God's grace and may you be another Sita." A contrasting tradition associates woman with power and strength: the goddess Durga-Kali representing Shakti, the dynamic power of the universe and a symbol of cosmic energy. In that model are many female political leaders of twentieth-century India--Sarojini Naidu (1879-1949), Vijaya Lakshmi Pandit (b. 1900), and Indira Gandhi (b. 1917). These are women of strength and resistance, articulate public champions of their chosen causes, and their lives are often suggested as patterns for young women in modern India. The Western view of human rights is not especially evident as an essential element in either the behavior of the traditionally submissive woman or in the political evolution of the twentieth-century leader.

III. *The Impact of the West*

From the first contact with imperial Europe in the early sixteenth century through two hundred years of direct and indirect British rule (ending in 1947), India was increasingly affected by Western ideas. In 1858 the British Government took over the interests of the British East India Company and the empire began. During the next century the British ruled India in two administrative formats: direct government extended over approximately 60 per cent of India; and indirect government, exercised through local rulers, over the balance of the territory. Gradually, the British sought to extend their version of social rights to India. Among measures they introduced were the abolition of *suti* (widow immolation) by the 1850's, enactment of the Caste Disabilities Removal Act of 1850 (this prevented religious conversion resulting in the forfeiture of inheritance), the Hindu Widow's Remarriage Act of 1856 (making intercaste marriages legal), and legal regulations providing special concessions for disadvantaged castes. These efforts were often better enforced in the directly governed areas and in urban regions, and their subcontinental impact was less than the scope of legislation suggests. More important perhaps was the fact that a section of the Indian nationalist leadership was influenced by

117

these ideas and began to accept or consider the validity of many of the propositions contained in the Western human rights concept.

The Western impact and its impetus for modernization (essentially a combination of Western ideas and socio-economic organization) also produced a degree of administrative centralization that persisted after national independence was achieved in 1947. This has generated tensions between urban and rural segments of society that are, at best, a struggle for accommodation within the hierarchy of national priorities and, at worst, a serious conflict of visions and policies. For the past several decades the modernizing city, with about 20 per cent of India's current population of approximately 650 million, has sought to extend and impose its values (including some ideas of Western human rights) on the traditional way of life of the rural areas. Here, in 600,000 villages, are the bulk of the Indian people, those whose lives are conditioned by the dynamics of tradition, resistant to socio-cultural change, maintaining the ordered universe of proven historic verities. The influence of the "cities" is enhanced by the instruments of modern government--mass education, a national political system, communications, and other penetrations into the hinterland. With them come elements of human rights, Western style.

Two major thrusts symbolize the growing impact of "city"-initiated, Western-rooted influences:

First, the human rights reforms introduced into modern India. The constitution of 1950 guaranteed equality before the law, the Untouchability (Offenses) Act of 1955 made caste discrimination a criminal offense, the Special Marriage Act of 1954 and the Hindu Marriage and Divorce Act of 1955 made divorce easier and enforced monogamy. The Hindu

Succession Act of 1956 gave women equal inheritance and other rights. Similar legislation in recent years has advanced the secularization of civil law and the rights of women, and introduced penalties for social discrimination. Electoral laws and regular national elections have made political rights a reality.

Second, the gradual change that Hinduism is undergoing. In the past century or so, several reformers (e.g., Ram Mohan Roy, Dayananda Saraswathi, Vivekananda in the nineteenth century; Gandhi, Aurobindo in the twentieth century) have sought to divorce Hinduism from its own social tradition and to disassociate the faith from those practices inconsistent with Western socio-political ideas. Although their success in changing attitudes has been limited, they have had a major influence on the power centers of modern India.

However, legal modernization and religious reform are slow processes in a democratic environment. Making law a reality takes considerable time, enforcement is often difficult and has met with much resistance or evasion--and could create consequences contrary to Western expectations in the human rights area. Frequently, the adoption of Western-oriented concepts, which produce liberalizing results when applied in Western societies, has produced very different results when applied in non-Western societies.

IV. *Implications*

There are three questions that a current analysis of human rights in Indian political culture provokes:

1. *Has the discussion of human rights (in the Western conceptual context) any relevance to Indian political culture?* In historical perspective and for many Indians today such a discussion may have

minimal meaning. Rights and entitlements were determined by different values in the past, much of their influence endures, and economic urgencies often dictate immediate priorities. Yet, there is sufficient evidence to indicate that Western attitudes about the individual and his or her rights do have a growing relevance in India. These attitudes now frequently determine major events in Indian public life; one of the lessons of the recent Indian experience is that political education need not coincide with formal education. Basic to understanding Indian political culture, both present and future, is an appreciation of the development of the Indian tradition and the current interaction between its themes and Western ideas of human rights.

2. *Will social and economic modernization enhance human rights?* The expectation of many Western analysts is that these modernizations will bring greater liberalization, more Western-patterned political democracy, and further extensions of individual rights. India, in this first phase of nationhood, has promoted the advancement of human rights. However, grafting Western notions of political liberty onto traditional Hindu collective social forms may result in a modernizing, but authoritarian-oriented society in which economic and social rights may be pursued more vigorously than political rights. An examination of contemporary politics in India leaves open this possibility.

3. *What can the United States do in the area of human rights in India?* The Carter administration, coming to office in early 1977, at approximately the same time as the Desai regime in India, developed a policy supportive of the Janata government. Addressing the Indian Parliament in early January, 1978, President Carter congratulated the Janata government for restoring civil liberties.

In my view such policies and statements reflect a serious misreading of the Indian political culture and do not enhance either the cause of human rights or longer term United States interests. They ignore, among other things, the fact that the Janata Party was able to win an election only because a free and fair election was held by the government of Indira Gandhi--a fact that Prime Minister Callaghan recognized in a similar address to the Indian legislature in early February, 1978. Perhaps the best role for the United States in the Indian situation is to refrain from political rhetoric indicative of a certain partisanship and to recognize that economic conditions are a key to the evolution of political circumstances in the immediate future.

A final reflection. Do Western concepts of human rights have to be expressed through Western-type, liberal democratic political structures? At the present level of global political evolution there is little to suggest the contrary. However, it may be that the special accommodative genius of Hindu culture could create a new synthesis and produce the type of adjustment it has achieved in other areas. Perhaps both Indian political culture and Western political ideals can transcend their historical constrictions, taking lessons from the ways in which India has already adopted and adapted forms of democracy in the past three decades.

Bibliography

Ashby, Philip H. *Modern Trends in Hinduism.* New York: Columbia University Press, 1974.

Buultjens, Ralph. *Rebuilding the Temple--Tradition and Change in Modern Asia.* Maryknoll, N.Y.: Orbis Books, 1974.

Chethimattam, John. *Patterns of Indian Thought.* Maryknoll, N.Y.: Orbis Books, 1971.

Embree, Ainslie T., ed. *The Hindu Tradition.* New York: Random House/Modern Library, 1966.

Ghurye, G.S. *Caste and Race in India.* Bombay: Popular Books, 1969.

Glaser, Kurt and Possony, Stefan. *Victims of Politics--the State of Human Rights.* New York: Columbia University Press, 1979.

Radhakrishnan, S. *The Hindu Way of Life.* New York: Macmillan Co., 1963.

Smith, Donald Eugene. *India as a Secular State.* Princeton: Princeton University Press, 1963.

Srinivas, M.N. *Social Change in Modern India.* Berkeley: University of California Press, 1971.

Varma, V.P. *Modern Indian Political Thought.* Agra: Agarwal Educational Pubs., 1974.

Ward, Barbara. *India and the West.* New York: W.W. Norton, 1964.

Wilkins, W.J. *Hindu Mythology.* Calcutta: Rupa Paperbacks, 1975.

HUMAN RIGHTS IN AFRICAN POLITICAL CULTURE

ASMAROM LEGESSE

When we speak of human rights today, we generally
mean rights as they are enshrined in the Universal
Declaration of Human Rights. Unfortunately, this
particular document is not entirely satisfactory because it is a statement of values that derive
directly from the liberal democracies of the Western
world. The basic document was formulated before
most of the Third World, and nearly all of Africa,
achieved independence. As a result, the Declaration is universal in its intent but not in its
derivation.[1]

If a conception of human rights is to command the
loyalty of all nations, Western and non-Western, it
is essential that the underlying ideas be examined
in a crosscultural framework free from the implications of the *mission civilizatrice*, the supremacist
perspective that elevates one culture above all
others. Any system of ideas that claims to be universal must contain critical elements in its fabric
that are avowedly of African, Latin American, or
Asian derivation. We have no difficulty identifying
those ideas in the Universal Declaration of Human
Rights that derive from the Magna Carta, the American and French revolutions, and the constitutions
of the modern liberal democracies. Does anything
in that document derive from Africa? If not, why
should Africans see it as *their* charter and not as

123

an alien system of ideas that is, once again, imposed upon them from without?

There are two problems that stand in the way of
a meaningful dialogue on the issue of human rights.
The first is a problem of communication: Different
societies formulate their conception of human
rights in diverse cultural idioms. The second is a
problem of hierarchy of values: When forced to
choose between basic values, societies rank them
differently. On neither score can cultures claim
inherent superiority over others without relapsing
into the crassest forms of cultural supremacist
thinking of the Victorian variety. They merely
postpone the resolution.

One critical difference between African and Western traditions concerns the importance of the human
individual. In the liberal democracies of the Western world the ultimate repository of rights is the
human person. The individual is held in a virtual-
ly sacralized position. There is a perpetual, and
in our view obsessive, concern with the dignity of
the individual, his worth, personal autonomy, and
property. The individual is celebrated in folklore
and literature and is portrayed as fighting to preserve his domain against the oppressive forces of
society and the threatening forces of nature. Nothing is more despicable to the Westerner than societies that force individuals to be lost in the
"faceless crowd."

No aspect of Western civilization makes an
African more uncomfortable than the concept of the
sacralized individual whose private wars against
society are celebrated. If we turn the situation
around and view it from an African perspective, the
individual who is fighting private wars against his
society is no hero. That is precisely the kind of
individual whom an African would accuse of witch-

craft. In Ethiopia the extreme individualist is called *buda* and ostracized.

What kind of heroes does Africa celebrate? The question cannot be answered directly because it assumes that Africa has heroes just as the West does. In Africa heroism itself is suspect. Put in a different way, the very idea of advertising cultural values by personifying them in the lives of individuals is a very strange idiom to an African. Heroism is a phenomenon of the Indo-European world, and it is directly connected with the concept of the sacralized individual.

The heart of African culture is egalitarian and antiheroic in character. In response to this generalized statement my anthropological colleagues are likely to rush off to the Human Relations Area Files--that magnificent catalogue of human cultures-- and count the number of African societies that are egalitarian and those that are not. The point that I am making here refers to a reality deeper than can be revealed in statistical frequencies. Most African cultures, whether they are formally egalitarian or hierarchical, have mechanisms of distributive justice that ensure that individuals do not deviate so far from the norm that they can overwhelm the society. This is the factor that was widespread throughout precolonial Africa and served as the cornerstone of African morality. A few examples drawn from traditional African societies will suffice.

Among the Anuak who live on the border of the Sudan and Ethiopia the chief is elected by his community on the basis of his wealth and leadership qualities. Once installed, the chief is expected to feast his subjects so often that his resources are soon depleted and he is impoverished. He then returns to his original status of common citizen and another wealthy candidate is put in his place.

The Anuak people are more extreme than most in using political office as an instrument of redistributive justice. Most African kings and chiefs were expected to use their wealth for the welfare of their subjects. The emperors and noblemen of Ethiopia were expected to die in poverty after lavishing their subjects with gifts and bequeathing their estates to the churches and monasteries. The same idea occurs again and again in most of the monarchies of Africa.

Among the Nyakyusa of Tanzania local communities organize themselves into cooperative work crews that ensure that every farm is brought up to the community standard. The laggard is coaxed to raise his performance to an acceptable level. Nobody is allowed to live off the effort of others. At the same time, outstanding individuals who outperform their neighbors and who do nothing to share their good fortune are psychologically penalized in the sense that they are often made the object of witchcraft accusations. In short, the African work ethic as reflected in this society tolerates neither extreme.[2]

Among the Amhara of northern Ethiopia there is a system of land tenure that illustrates one aspect of the African concept of distributive justice. Land is divided equally among sons and daughters. It is passed on from generation to generation by fathers and mothers separately. Individuals hold land, but the descent group owns it collectively and in perpetuity. All the Christian peasantry has access to land. It is neither possible to accumulate land nor is it possible to be deprived of it. The poor cannot fall out at the bottom and the rich cannot break out at the top. Nobody, including the emperor, could deprive the peasant of his right to land. It is this institution that en-

126

shrines the most basic idea of "human rights." Land tenure is so central to Amhara culture that their fundamental notions of morality derive from that system.[3]

The principle of distributive justice also extends into the area of generational relationships. Many African societies have age organizations that break up the community into several age groups. Each group is internally governed by egalitarian rules of conduct. However, the inequality of different age groups poses a problem. Age clearly confers authority and prestige and each age group tends to dominate and exploit the age group below it. To mitigate this pattern of dominance the oldest generation establishes a formal alliance with the youngest and both stand in opposition to the middle generation, i.e., the generation that is in the prime of life and, if left unchecked, tends to overwhelm the very young and the very old. Thus what is inherently a relationship of inequality is converted into a relationship of balanced opposition.[4]

It is not possible in the context of a short essay such as this to do justice to the great diversity of African cultures and abstract from them the shared ethical foundations. Many studies have been carried out that suggest that distributive justice, in the economic and political spheres, is the cardinal ethical principle that is shared by most Africans.[5] In particular, one broadly based comparative investigation entitled "Checks on the Abuse of Political Authority in Some African States," by John Beattie[6] shows how widespread these ideas are in the traditional socio-political systems. Africans set limits on political and economic inequality, not because they are underdeveloped, but because they have evolved the most elaborate and highly effective institutions designed

127

to inhibit schisms between the rich and the poor, the men of power and those they govern.

The centrality of the ethic of distributive justice is, of course, the reason why Africans are so reluctant to celebrate individual achievement and to use a heroic cultural idiom to symbolize their values. The purpose is not to dangle before the eyes of the many the accomplishments of the few, and thus keep the underprivileged hoping for respite; the purpose is, rather, to convert individual assets into communal benefits.

If Africans were the sole authors of the Universal Declaration of Human Rights, they might have ranked the rights of communities above those of individuals, and they might have used a cultural idiom fundamentally different from the language in which the ideas are now formulated.

The worst violations of human rights in history were those directed against entire peoples. The decimation of native Americans in North and South America, the millions of lives lost in the African slave trade and the subsequent colonization of the continent, and the Armenian and Jewish holocausts in this century were all violations of peoples' rights on a massive scale. Today there are the so-called "minorities" in all nation-states who are brutally violated or reduced to second-class citizenship because their racial or cultural identity does not conform to the dominant national cultures. In this regard, the liberal democracies of the Western world have gone a long way toward offering a modicum of legal protection to their minorities, although culturally they are still extremely intolerant toward them.

Part of the problem is the fact that it is nation-states that sponsored the human rights movement and it is also nation-states that are most often the violators. In the absence of a supranational body that could adjudicate the conduct of states, there is little hope that international laws, declarations, or covenants will be effective.

There is some hope that moral pressure exerted through international bodies and voluntary associations might have some influence. To date it is not at all clear that such pressure has made a significant difference. No country has experienced more intense and more sustained pressure than South Africa in regard to its apartheid policy and the practice of keeping the African population thoroughly balkanized and exploited. Nonetheless, these policies continue unabated and, if anything, Afrikaner nationalism has become more deeply entrenched.[7]

It is also possible that some states will take it upon themselves to police the conduct of their neighbors. That is the posture of the United States at the present time. Similarly, Sweden has during the last ten years used its international aid program to pressure the recipient countries to introduce legal reform and to prevent recipients from using the assistance to exacerbate further existing social inequalities. Tanzania has actively supported liberation movements in the racist states of Southern Africa and overtly criticized the conduct of Idi Amin in Uganda. These are all bold steps taken sporadically by particular states in defense of human rights. On the whole, however, these actions are not institutionalized and appear to be the product of the moral convictions of particular leaders.

The problem is deeper than the present underdeveloped state of international law. The real problem has to do with the fact that the most outspoken champions of human rights--the liberal democracies of the Western world--are themselves often violators of human rights. Their pattern of violation is not as obvious as that of Hitler's Germany or Verwoerd's South Africa. It is, nonetheless, an endemic problem that constitutes a threat to the rest of mankind. Their offense is simply the fact that they are still engaged in a civilizing mission vis-à-vis the rest of mankind. They still define the problem of human rights as one of lack of proper political education in the underdeveloped world. They have already succeeded in writing most of their values and code of ethics into the Universal Declaration. Hence, the human rights movement faces the danger of becoming an instrument of cultural imperialism. To the extent that the West fails to realize that other cultural traditions may be as deeply committed to rights, although approaching it from a different ethical perspective, to that extent the movement rests on false premises and tends to legitimize the behavior it seeks to eradicate.

Two of the greatest thinkers in Africa, Julius Nyerere and Leopold Sedar Senghor, have devoted much thought to the African cultural foundations and their relevance to the evolution of national and universal cultures. Both men have headed relatively stable African states in which the rights of peoples have been recognized and are respected. There is a direct causal link between these leaders' recognition of their African roots and their polities' recognition of all the "minorities" that make up these nations. What is Africa if not a vast agglomeration of "minorities" who collectively make up the "majority"? Majoritarian thinking itself is, in the final analysis, a variety of supremacist thought based on the crude premise of the "survival of the biggest."

Tanzania is a nation of "minorities," none of whom are relegated to second-class citizenship. Nyerere himself comes from a small tribe that cannot aspire to dominate the other peoples in the country. Nyerere has made the equality of peoples, including non-African immigrants, the cornerstone of his philosophy of African Socialism:

The essence of socialism is the practical acceptance of human equality. That is to say, every man's equal right to a decent life before any individual has a surplus above his needs; his equal right to participate in Government; and his equal responsibility to work and con- tribute to the society to the limit of his ability.[8]

He is also aware of the fact that values often clash even in the best of ethical worlds, and when they do, the priorities must be unambiguous:

Inherent in the Arusha Declaration, therefore, is a rejection of the concept of national grandeur as distinct from the well-being of its citizens, and a rejection too of material wealth for its own sake. It is a commitment to the belief that there are more important things in life than the amassing of riches, and that if the pursuit of wealth clashes with things like human dignity and social equality, then the latter will be given priority.[9]

When Idi Amin took power in the neighboring state of Uganda and began his reign of terror, Nyerere was openly critical of his policies and practices. The extreme atrocities to which Ugandans were subjected were deeply offensive to Africans everywhere, and yet few African leaders were willing to condemn Amin. It is therefore fitting that Tanzania should be the scourge that finally rid

Uganda of Idi Amin.

Equality of all peoples is the highest value
that Nyerere has advocated throughout his career.
He is perpetually opposed to the rise of élitism
and the establishment of privileged classes. If
Nyerere has endured over the years while so many
other African contemporaries have fallen, it is
partly because he has achieved a level of ethical
validity that is based, not on force, but on consent. He is legitimate in a sense that so many of
the police states in Africa are not.

Another leading thinker in Africa is Leopold
Sedar Senghor. He also has had to use little force
to keep himself in power. He has inspired a whole
generation of Africans to contemplate their tradition and to use it effectively in building their
nations. He has acknowledged the Hamitic populations in the country and offered them full partnership. He is aware of the fact that black racism is
no less pernicious than any other kind of racism.
Senghor has risen above the "I am blacker than
thou" type of petty ethnocentrism and declared
Senegal to be an Afro-Berber civilization. To him
the mixing of cultures (*mestissage culturelle*) in
the construction of national culture is an essential
step. The philosophy of *négritude* does not exclude
Hamitic Africa. It incorporates the Hamitic world
and elements of European civilization as well. The
philosophy is neither Christian nor Muslim in its
orientation. It draws its inspiration from both.
It is, in other words, a nonsupremacist program of
cultural integration.

The entire *négritude* movement that Senghor
launched is a movement of cultural affirmation and
an attempt to let the world know that a study of
African values should be as important to the formulation of universal ideals as any other culture.

In this venture Africa is up against the formidable barrier of Euro-American ethnocentrism and its view of the world as consisting of high and low cultures, great and small religions. Senghor captures the paradoxes of European ethnocentrism in the following passage:

> Strange people, the French, so seductive, and sometimes so irritating. I have traveled widely across Europe and have not known a people as human as them....I know of no other people more tyrannical in their love of Man. They want bread for all, culture for all, liberty for all, but this liberty, this culture, this bread shall be *French*.[10]

The paradox that he examines here suggests that it is possible to be universalistic and ethnocentric at one and the same time. The essence of the philosophy of *négritude* is that it recognizes the deepest values shared by Africans and seeks to build upon these values by amalgamating them with elements drawn from other cultures, particularly those that do not violate the basic ethical premises of African civilization.

A few years ago I concluded the study of an African culture--the Boran of southern Ethiopia-- with the following words:

> *We* study African cultures so that they may live and grow to become the enduring foundation of a distinctive African civilization. In that process of growth every culture has something vital to offer. Man's wider cultural identities must be allowed to grow, not by the predatory expansion of one civilization but by the complementary integration of many diverse cultures. No human community, however humble, should be forced to give up its cultural identity without

making a critical contribution to the larger reality of which it becomes a part. That remains true whether the larger reality is national culture, pan-African culture, or universal culture.[11]

In other words, the universalizing process itself must rest on a premise of equality of all cultures and *overtly* incorporate elements drawn from Africa, Asia, and Latin America. Only then can the peoples of the Third World give up part of their cultural sovereignty, secure in the knowledge that their culture lives on in the fabric of universalism.

It is a truism to say that the world is becoming a single interdependent community. If by saying so we mean high-speed aircraft, instantaneous satellite communication, and a worldwide network of markets, then we are stating the obvious. If on the other hand we mean that the interconnected world must also share a single cultural umbrella of Euro-American derivation, then we are still in the colonial era. Cultural genocide is no less pernicious than physical genocide. A people deprived of their culture can die just as surely as a people whose material resource base has suddenly collapsed. That is the threat that the liberal democracies of the Western world pose to the rest of mankind. So long as they seek to civilize the world from a wholly supremacist perch, the problem will endure.

Under the leadership of Jimmy Carter the United States has now become a champion of human rights worldwide. This attitude is a definite improvement over the opportunism of earlier periods. For the first time high principles and ethical standards have been permitted to influence foreign policy, and, accordingly, assistance has been withdrawn from nations that clearly violate the international Bill of Rights. This magnificent venture can be meaningful only if a serious dialogue is main-

tained with the Third World with the aim of re-
defining and thus universalizing the Bill of Rights.

It is also necessary for the United States to be
vigilant about violations of human rights at home.
It is easy to dismiss one's own atrocities as minor
aberrations. So long as black Americans continue
to be a cheap and disposable labor reserve that
serves as a buffer for the vacillating labor market;
so long as impoverished populations remain locked
in ghettoes, deprived of the fundamental right to
earn a living--to that degree the United States
violates the Bill of Rights. To call this the
problem of "unemployment" is, in Senghor's vivid
phrase, to "gargle a formula." Before America con-
demns South Africa for its racist policies, America
must reexamine its own ghettoes. The fact that the
American ghetto is maintained by informal procedures and the South African Bantustan is maintained
by law does not, in the final analysis, make much
difference.

It is important to stress that the problem of
cultural dominance across national boundaries has a
strange way of reversing its course and emerging
within the national boundaries as well. Europe's intolerance toward other cultures during the era of
imperialism translated itself locally into national
intolerance toward "subcultures." The more avid
the drive toward empire, the more supremacist the
premise of national integration and the more likely
that the nation will, sooner or later, face the resurgence of cultures once forcefully rubbed out of
existence for the greater glory of the nation.
Britain is the epitome of a once dominant nation
that is now looking inward, reexamining the very
structure of national life and restructuring the
position of the subdominant nationalities. That is
the irony of cultural domination.

The civilizing mission of an earlier era has proved to be a bankrupt philosophy. What Senghor and Nyerere have now proposed is not a slightly altered and Africanized version of the *mission civilizatrice*. It is an entirely novel conception of cultural evolution, one that is wholly free from the presuppositions of cultural dominance. The "civilized world," which is still paying the price of an earlier pattern of supremacist development, would do well to take from Third World thinkers the concept of the *equality of human cultures* and use that concept as a fundamentally new basis for cultural integration.

Notes

1. United Nations, *The Universal Declaration of Human Rights* (A/1311), 1950; and *United Nations Actions in the Field of Human Rights*, Twenty-Fifth Anniversary of the Universal Declaration of Human Rights, 1974.

2. Monica Wilson, *Good Company* (London: Oxford University Press, 1951).

3. Allan Hoben, *Land Tenure Among the Amhara of Ethiopia* (Chicago: University of Chicago Press, 1973); and Asmarom Legesse, "Post-Feudal Society, Capitalism and Revolution," paper presented to the Second Leo Frobenius Symposium, Dakar, Senegal, March 15, 1979.

4. Wilson, op. cit.; V. W. Turner, "Spatial Separation of Generations in Ndembu Village Structure," *Africa*, 25 (1955): 122-36; and Asmarom Legesse, *Gada: Three Approaches to the Study of African Society* (New York: Free Press, 1973).

5. Edward E. Evans-Pritchard, *The Nuer* (London: Oxford University Press, 1940); Max Gluckman, *Custom and Conflict in Africa* (Oxford: Blackwell, 1955); and Julius Nyerere, "Ujamaa: The Basis of African Socialism," in *African Socialism*, ed. W.H. Friedland (Stanford, Calif.: Stanford University Press, 1962).

6. John Beattie, "Checks on the Abuse of Political Authority in Some African States," in *Comparative Political Systems*, eds. R. Cohen and J. Middleton (New York: Natural History Press, 1967).

7. Barbara Rogers, *Divide and Rule: South Africa's Bantustans* (London: International Defense and Aid Fund, 1976).

8. Julius Nyerere, *Uhuru na Ujamaa: Freedom and Socialism* (London: Oxford University Press, 1968),

p. 325.

9. Ibid., p. 316.

10. Leopold Sedar Senghor, *Liberté I: Négritude et Humanisme* (Paris: Edition du Seuil), vol. 1, p. 98; translation mine.

11. Legesse, *Gada*, p. 291.

HUMAN RIGHTS IN ISLAMIC POLITICAL CULTURE

JAMES P. PISCATORI

Allāh, like all great gods, affirms the dignity of
man: "We have called noble (*karramunā*) the sons of
Adam."[1] Over time, however, civilizational rival-
ries and theological sensitivities obscured the
simple clarity of this revelation by generating two
competing and equally misleading views of how
special man is to Islam. One view, encouraged from
the days of Crusader propaganda, accuses Muslims of
basely discriminating among men and inflicting
horrors on the unbeliever. The begrudgingly
respectful description of the brave Saracen fighter
in *La Chanson de Roland* soon degenerated in European literature into the vulgar stereotype of the
Moor and Turk who would rape and decapitate as soon
as offer the five daily prayers.[2] The opposing
view, developed by admirers of Islam over the centuries, contends that it, more than other religions,
tolerates individual differences and is relatively
free of racial and ethnic prejudices. Inspired by
the Qur'ānic injunction that men are set apart only
by their piety, Ibn Ḥazm wrote in the eleventh century: "God has decreed that the most devout is the
noblest even if he be a Negress's bastard, and that

*The author wishes to thank Lisa deFilippis for her
assistance in the preparation of this essay.*

the sinner and unbeliever is at the lowest level even if he be the son of prophets."[3] More recent adherents of the faith make it seem that theirs is a society of real interracial harmony and enviable fraternity.[4]

Neither image, of course, is correct. The first, denouncing the cruelties of Muslims, fails to take note that if it is true that Muslim warriors were often unrestrained in dealing with the infidels, it is also true that they gave as they received. Recalling Richard the Lionhearted's decapitation of 2,700 prisoners of war at 'Akka in 1191, we would realize that not only Muslims were inhumane; remembering Clement's 1311 decree prohibiting Muslim services, outlawing the pilgrimage to Makka, and proscribing the name of Muḥammad in Christian nations, we would see that intolerance was not an exclusively Eastern phenomenon.[5] The second image, while extolling Islamic egalitarianism, fails to explain why few political leaders, in fact, rose from the ranks of the ethnic minorities. There is little reassurance in the self-conscious way that Ibn Ḥazm and others offer respect for blacks as an almost incredulous example of Islam's openness; as Bernard Lewis argues, we can never be convinced that they themselves believe in the point they make for effect.[6] The flattering image, finally, cannot dispel the fact that the slaves of Muslims were precisely that--so much property to man the armies and to mine the resources of the empires. The thought of the Zanj working the salt flats of southern Mesopotamia under the most primitive conditions stands in vivid juxtaposition to the idea that Islam, unlike the West, has avoided the uncivilized.

I. *Classical Islam*

Islam, however, ought not to be viewed from its
historical record, which inevitably will be found
wanting, but from the values it commends to all men
in every age. As a religious and political code
Islam brought radically new standards to apply to
the polytheistic, tribal Arabian peninsula of the
seventh century. For the Badawīn and townsmen
there, the Revelation transmitted through Muḥammad
in Arabic represented their own "leap in being."[7]
It was, indeed, a revolutionary event that induced
new ways of looking at man. Because government's
purpose was now to serve Allāh's will and to help
men to do the same, the individual, in return for
his obedience, received assurance that he was not
the natural prey of self-regulating rulers. With
the advent of Islam as well it became possible for
men to tie their identity to a communal group based
on fraternity and equality in the faith. Membership in the Islamic *umma* freed the individual from
the narrow confines of tribal kinship (*'aṣabiyya*)
and allowed him to appeal to the larger community
for comfort and support. Finally, Islam introduced
specific reforms to correct unjust practices of the
period preceding it. For example, infanticide,
which was particularly applied to girl babies, was
vigorously condemned as a "great sin" (*khiṭan
kabīran*).[8] In addition, the Qur'ān, imposing a new
limit of four wives, enjoined that they be treated
justly, and it circumscribed the ability of husbands to employ solemn oaths as a pretext for denying their wives conjugal privileges. It also set
definite limits to the cycle of murder and revenge
that traditionally exposed the individual to the
perils of blood feuds.[9]

Though Islam brought a new order, its merits derive from the contrast with the pre-Islamic "Days
of Ignorance." Relative to existing mores, Islamic

141

humanism marked a distinct improvement in respect for the individual. It would be wrong, however, to conclude that Islam also introduced a concept of human rights comparable to that commonly understood today. If the concept means that all men have inviolable freedoms that are their natural due and are independent of governmental approval, then it is an idea largely alien to Islam. There is, in fact, no equivalent doctrine to that of the Rights of Man that developed in the eighteenth-century West. Several reasons account for the absence of such a notion.

First, the idea of rights is more applicable to God than man, for Islam is a civilization predicated on the belief that all things are the inalienable property of Allāh. The rights of God are comprehensive and inclusive: "It is He who has created for you all that is in the earth, then he turned to heaven...."[10] As a consequence, Islamic jurisprudence extensively elaborates the duties (farūḍ) of men, but there is scant reference to their rights. The "rights" that are mentioned, constituting the ḥuqūq al-ādamiyyīn, are hardly equivalent to modern human rights, since they apply to specific claims in penal law. According to the Sharī'a, certain crimes, such as drinking wine and adultery, are so offensive that the prescribed penalties constitute the ḥuqūq Allāh, or claims of God, and hence cannot be avoided. Theft and false witness, however, because they affect other individuals, may give rise to private claims, although they are not automatically prosecuted.[11] Thus, these claims, of God and of men, are "rights" only in a particular and limited sense.

Second, in Islam, man's existence is not the sufficient condition of his due, as it is in French revolutionary and Jeffersonian liberal thought. Rather, it is man's relationship to his Creator

that is the predominant factor, and the message
given to Muḥammad leaves no doubt that the relationship must be one of complete submission. Men are
to become the slaves of Allāh (*'ibād Allāh*), and
whosoever do not become the Lord's servants have no
legitimate claims against him. In this regard,
man's submission to God's will is the necessary
condition of his due, but there is no further understanding that it is also sufficient. The "rights
of man" in Islam, then, are neither intrinsic nor
universal: They depend on man's acts rather than
inhere in his existence; they are applicable to one
who submits--literally, the Muslim--while they are
less, if at all, applicable to one who does not
submit.

Finally, in Islam, the individual's due is also
conditioned on his obedience to government. It is
a divinely ordained obligation,[12] with rulers having
their own duty to suppress disorder and injustice
so that men can get on with their religious worship.
The intimate Islamic connection of religious and
political functions, unlike the Christian West's
dualism of Caesar's and God's due, obviates the
need for a rival--ecclesiastical or other--institu-
tion to check the validity and the power of the
regime. Because religious and political authorities
join to interpret God's word, provisions for governmental limitations would seem, at the least, ir-
relevant and, at most, offensive. Though Islam, as
a consequence, lacks a concept of institutional
balances,[13] it is not a political theory of tyranny;
to be sure, there are clear prophetic traditions
that obligate men to obey only the good. There is,
however, a fundamental difference from Western
thought with its Gelasian-like division of the
secular and churchly: Islamic monism, whereby government is dedicated to the temporal *and* spiritual
welfare of its citizens, does not give rise to a
theory of civil rights for the protection of the

143

individual.

There are, then, several basic differences between classical Islam and the philosophy behind the modern human rights movement. Simply put, Islamic theory does not present a notion of the rights of the individual. Rights do not attach to men *qua* men; they belong not to the product but, eternally and indisputably, to the Creator. For this reason and because man's due is conditional--on his submission to God and to God's representatives--it is more appropriate to refer to the *privileges* of man. Man's due is not universally the same or automatically owed, but it is variable according to religious belief and dependent on good behavior.

In addition to the grand, philosophical differences there are important, specific differences between classical Islam and the human rights advanced in international forums today. Perhaps the most celebrated and the most controversial example is women's rights. There is no doubt that, according to the Sharī'a, women do not receive privileges equal to those of men. It is true that women deserve honor as children of God and special protection as mothers. Yet it is also true that Islamic law demands that women be obedient for this protection and even permits men to punish for disobedience.[14] There are as well clear inequalities in marital privileges. While a Muslim man may marry an unbelieving woman, the obverse is strictly proscribed; in fact, the marriage of a Muslim woman to a non-Muslim man is without legal effect.[15] In addition, there is little flexibility in divorce proceedings for the wife. While in principle the husband may not deprive his wife of gifts he gave her during the marriage, a judge may qualify the principle, if its application would prompt a violent response from the husband.[16] In general, a man may divorce without judicial action and as easily as a thrice-repeated denunciation of the marriage bonds (ṭalāq), and he may remarry almost without restriction. A woman, however, does not have the same privilege of divorcing her husband. She may buy her freedom (khul'), or she may seek annulment (faskh), if she can prove the impotence, repulsive illness, nonsupport, or repeated cruelty of her husband. But these are difficult charges to prove, and they must be evaluated by a judge. Furthermore, when a woman resumes an unmarried state for whatever reason, she may not remarry until after going through a celibate period ('idda). There is in Islamic law, finally, a normative weighting that makes the testimony of a man worth twice that of a female witness and his inheritance double that of a woman. God has made clear the latter teaching "lest you go astray."[17]

Another major area of disagreement is freedom of religion. The Qur'ān vigorously denounces those who renounce Islam, for "the Devil has seduced them" away from the true faith.[18] The major historical example is the revolt of the tribes after Muhammad's death in 632 A.D. Abu Bakr, and jurists since then, condemned secession from Islam (ridda) as doubly heinous: It not only is a violation of the compact of submission made with Allāh, but it is also a breach of contract with his representatives on earth. It is, then, an offense both against God and against the state; it is both apostasy and treason. Far from having the right to become a non-Muslim, the Muslim faces the death penalty as a sanction for such a change. "He who changes his religion, must be killed," the Prophet said.[19] Islamic rulers, moreover, may wage jihād against a group of apostates who aid and abet the enemies of Islam. Scholars, agreeing that the traitors must either resubmit to Islam or submit to major combat, disagree on the ius in bello that applies. The Hanafīs, for example, differ from others in arguing that the wives and

145

children of apostates become slaves or spoils of war.[20]

It is not surprising that such religious sensitivity also translates into an inequality of status between the believers and the unbelievers. While all the latter are blameworthy for enticing the former toward hell,[21] not all unbelievers are equally odious. Polytheists are particularly objectionable because of their substitution of multiple gods for the one God. The law is clear on the treatment Muslims must mete out to them: "slay them (*qutulū*) wherever you may find them."[22] The non-Muslim monotheists fare better, for as people adhering to revealed scriptures (*ahl al-kitāb*), they deserve protection in return for a commitment to live peacefully in the Islamic community. There are ample historical examples, from the Prophet's compacts with the people of al-Madīna, Najrān, and al-'Aqaba, to the ordinances of 'Umar, to the *millet* system of the Ottomans, which testify to a well-developed jurisprudence on the subject. *Dhimmīs*, or the protected non-Muslims, when they pay a tax (*jizya*) to the Islamic state, are allowed to follow their own laws of personal status, to own property, to travel without restriction, except into the area of the holy cities, and to practice their religion. Muslim authorities, however, may prohibit them from marrying Muslims, engaging in certain business activities, inheriting from Muslims, showing disrespect to Islam, carrying arms, and worshiping in an obviously public manner. The authorities may also require that they wear apparel different from, and live in houses smaller than, those of the Muslim citizens. Reviewing these restrictions, Majid Khadduri concludes that *dhimmīs* are second-class citizens[23] and Muhammad Talāt al-Ghunaymī that they are noncitizens in the Islamic polity.[24]

There is, finally, a distinction between the Islamic view of punishment and that held by many ad-

vocates of expanding human rights today. The Qur'ān
does provide for a form of *lex talionis*, though it
would be wrong to assume that Islamic jurists are
unanimous in their interpretation of it. The
Ḥanbalīs, for example, tend to be stricter constructionists than do scholars of the three other basic
legal traditions. In general, the Sharī'a provides for retaliation (*qiṣāṣ*) in murder cases,
whereby either a compensatory financial settlement
or the taking of someone's life is the prescribed
penalty.[25] The traditional punishment for theft is
the severance of a hand,[26] but scholars do not
agree that it applies to all robbery cases. There
is also a flogging penalty for adultery, after four
witnesses testify to its occurrence. If a witness
testifies falsely, he himself is to receive a flogging and be debarred as a credible witness in subsequent litigation.[27] In keeping with the religious and political nature of Islam, the purpose of
these punishments (*ḥudūd*) is twofold: to manifest
divine displeasure and to set a civic example.

II. *Islam in the Modern World*

The differences I have outlined do not discredit
Islam anymore than they flatter the prevailing
thinking on human rights. Indeed, a survey of
ancient and medieval thought will reveal its own
share of currently unpalatable ideas. Greek
political thought treats slaves as part of the
natural order, Judaic and New Testament scriptures
endorse harsh and retaliatory penalties, and vir-
tually every Western thinker who deals with the
subject, like Paul in Ephesians 5, teaches that
women must submit to male authority. But the proponents of the human rights covenants do not suggest that premodern thought does more than lay the
groundwork for the development of modern liberalism.
By way of contrast, Muslims, except for the
secularists, today propose that the Islam of

classical jurisprudence defines, or at least
qualifies, their approach to human rights.

The traditionalists center about the Persian
Gulf, where Saudi Arabia, the shaykhdoms, Pakistan,
and a significant movement in Iran are committed to
the continued application of the Sharī'a. Women's
privileges in divorce and inheritance are circumscribed in the Arabian peninsula, and a post-Shah
Iran may well follow suit. The military government
of General Zia has reinstituted the *ḥadd* penalties
in Pakistan, and Saudi Arabia long ago acquired
notoriety for its application of the sanctions of
classical law. The recent executions of two members of the royal family for murder and adultery
and the public floggings of British citizens engaged in selling alcohol to Muslims stand as evidence of the Saudi government's commitment to carry
out the letter of the law.[28] The Ayatollah Khomeini
has indicated that an "Islamic republic" of Iran
will be similarly faithful. The Saudis also re-
strict the practice of non-Islamic worship and prohibit non-Muslim entry to the holy area of Makka
and al-Madīna. Outside the Gulf, Libya has reverted
to applying the Sharī'a in inheritance privileges,
the prohibition of alcohol, and traditional punishments in limited circumstances.

It would be wrong, however, to conclude that the
Muslim world as a whole follows these examples.
There have been cultural changes, in fact, that have
given rise to Muslim loose constructionists who seek
to modernize their societies without discarding the
traditional legal sources. There is a built-in
flexibility to Islamic jurisprudence that allows
this course. Indeed, reformers are able to pick
and choose interpretations among four main schools,
to match Qur'ānic quote with quote or prophetic
tradition with tradition, and/or to invoke *ijtihād*,
or independent reasoning. Through these interpre-

148

tive means, and sometimes through executive fiat, several Islamic states have enacted legislation that substantially alters the lot of the individual from that expected under the classical law. Egypt changed its marriage laws in 1920, 1923, and 1929, and in 1956 it abrogated the Sharī'a courts. Jordan abandoned Hanafī-Ottoman law on the family in 1951, and Syria (1953), Tunisia (1957), Morocco (1959), Algeria (1959), Iraq (1959 and 1963), and South Yemen (1974) enacted new laws of personal status. Outside the Arab world, Pakistan established the Muslim Family Laws Ordinance of 1961; Iran, the Family Protection Acts of 1967 and 1975; and Somalia, the Family Law of 1975.[29]

There has been a marked improvement in the status of women in particular as a result of some of these laws. The Iranian, Pakistani, and Tunisian codes allow a wife to seek a divorce in a greater number of instances than the restrictive traditional law would allow. The Syrian and Moroccan enactments seek to protect the wife from her husband's arbitrary repudiation by limiting the conditions in which he can invoke $talāq$, and by attaching a financial penalty to an unwarranted repudiation. The Algerian, Iranian, Somali, and South Yemeni codes go even further in limiting the husband's traditional privileges by listing the permissible grounds of divorce for both man and wife. Syria, Morocco, Pakistan, and Iran have also severely restricted polygyny and justified their efforts to do so by noting the impossibility of fulfilling the Qur'ānic injunction that multiple wives be treated equally. Tunisia has gone the furthest in directly outlawing polygynous marriages. There have been, finally, a few--though not entirely successful--efforts to revise the traditional law of inheritance. Tunisia appealed to the opinion of three of the four legal schools in order to justify its 1959 enactment allowing daughters a greater

149

share, and Iraq, reflecting political and sectarian differences, has tried to reconcile the more liberal Shī'ī view on female inheritance with the traditional Sunnī one.[30]

.The nations of Islam today differ in more than domestic laws. There are also variations in the approach to the developing international law of human rights. No Islamic state voted against the Universal Declaration of Human Rights in 1948, but only eight states with Muslim majorities have become parties to the Covenants on Civil and Political Rights and on Economic, Social, and Cultural Rights: Iran, Iraq, Jordan, Lebanon, Libya, Mali, Syria, and Tunisia. A great deal of opposition to these texts is based on fear that they will intrude on sovereign prerogatives, but several Islamic states have rejected parts of them on Islamic grounds. Saudi Arabia, under Ambassador al-Bārūdī, has been especially active in opposing articles of the covenants because of their offensiveness to the traditional law.

Al-Bārūdī strenuously objected to the provision of the Universal Declaration and a draft article of the Covenant on Civil and Political Rights that would allow the right to change religion. He argued that this right would insult the world's Muslims, who are under an obligation not to leave their faith; it would invite missionaries into so sensitive an area as the holy Arabian peninsula; and it would contravene the Qur'ān, the law of some Islamic lands, and so violate the United Nations Charter's prohibition of interference in a state's domestic affairs. In the 1948 deliberations, Afghanistan, Iraq, Pakistan, and Syria joined Saudi Arabia in seeking to delete the proposed right, and when they failed, the latter criticized Lebanon, which voted in favor of the right, for an insensitivity to its own Muslim people.[31] During the later debates, al-Bārūdī reiterated the fundamental concern of some Muslims: "{The Saudi} Government could not support the text of Article 18 of the draft Covenant as formulated by the Committee on Human Rights since it would raise doubts in the minds of ordinary people to whom their religion {is} a way of life."[32]

There was also objection, somewhat incredibly, to the right of social security. The Saudis feared that it would obligate them to adopt a Western notion that was both unfamiliar and less comprehensive than the one Islam provides. The Sharī'a, they argued, establishes a kind of "social justice" based on the *zakāt* tax, the income from property endowments (*awqāf*), and the duty to assist the poor and the infirm. The international legal right, then, is undesirable because the Western system of social security finds an Islamic analogue that is also less complex and more efficient.[33]

Some Muslims, understandably, have argued against the declaration's and covenants' articles on women's rights. Prior to the 1961 adoption of the Muslim Family Law Ordinance, the Pakistani delegate, opposing the international legal provision recognizing equality of rights in marriage, had argued that strict equality would put women at a disadvantage because of their natural need of protection.[34] In the debates over the Universal Declaration in 1948 the Saudi ambassador stressed that Islam creates a system whereby marriage is a social contract guaranteeing wives property, inheritance, and compensation for divorce. Marriage, an area where "Islamic law was explicit on the smallest details," ought not to be burdened by international requirements that wives be of "full age" and have "equal rights";[35] both demands, the Saudi representative felt, betrayed a Western bias and ignored the internal safeguards of Islam. In a remarkable testa-

ment to his and his government's consistency of
thought, al-Bārūdī in 1975 said that he was "not
denying that some of the demands of women's movements in the Western world were understandable and
legitimate, but those movements were overzealous
in their action and wrongly assumed that their
values were suited to the entire world."[36]

III. Apologetics

It is obvious that there is no uniform Islamic
perspective on human rights today. There is,
rather, a multiplicity of perspectives, coalesced
loosely around traditionalism and modernism, which
account for the differing positions in domestic
legislation and toward international law held by
the Islamic states. Underpinning most of the current interpretations, however, is the common belief
that Islam must be defended against the intellectual arrogance of the West. So acute is the
resentment at liberalism's condescension that many
Muslims, traditionalist and modernist, feel that
counterattack is the surest defense. Far from draw-
ing the conclusion I have, that there are note-
worthy *differences* between the Islamic and general
approach, they conclude that the Islamic way is as
good or even better. The thought process is illustrative of an unobjective, damaging apologetics
manifested in every culture or nation seeking to
protect its reputation and honor; it is current in
Islamic intellectual life.

Wilfred Cantwell Smith and Sir Hamilton Gibb
have brilliantly warned us of the dangers of such
self-indulgent thought. Muslim apologetes, in
mounting an offensive against the West, whether it
be for its rapacious and retarding colonial policies
or its poor record on human rights, presume to
demonstrate the virtues of Islam. Instead, they
distort the record of the West and Islam for debat-

ing points. As well, they display, unwittingly though unmistakably, an inferiority complex, nourished steadily among Muslims since the advent of Western capitulations in the East, the Ottoman defeats at Karlowitz and Küchük Kainarja, and the Napoleonic invasion of Egypt. The following passage suggests this complex:

...'The right to life' has been given to man only by Islam.

If this right is ever mentioned in constitutions or declarations of some nations, then it is clearly implied that this right is only applicable to their citizens. Violations of this basic right by those who have put it in their constitutions are so evident all over the world, in Australia, in America, in Africa, in India against Muslims, in Asia and Europe.

It is only Islam which has given genuine respect to human life regardless of nationality, colour or race. No doubt that this is one of the numerous highlights of Islam which shows its universality and all-embracing nature.[38]

Not all Muslim writers are as defensive, but most would agree that Islam has an inherent concept of "human rights." Muḥammad Khalaf Allāh Aḥmad, for example, considers it an inevitable deduction from the basic Islamic principle of the unity of God. Because all creation is subservient to divine wish, Allāh's command for justice and equality translates into a set of individual rights that the Qur'ān and traditional legal sources promote and that are akin to those rights enshrined in international law today.[39] Khālid Isḥāq also finds textual support for the guaranteed rights of social security, responsible and limited government, protection, justice, privacy, employment, equality, property, political participation, and freedom of expression.[40]

153

It is a remarkable testament to the current attractiveness of human rights that such reputable Muslims find the idea and Islam compatible. But the compatibility is more a reaction to a universally acclaimed benign symbol than a description of Islamic theory, and the effort to assert it entails tortuous arguments. Al-Ghunaymī, for instance, argues at one point that "it is no exaggeration if we maintain that Islamic legal theory is far advanced, in the domain of human rights, to the standards which modern international law has attained." And yet, at another point, he denies the very basis of the current notion: "Human rights, as any right, are not absolute rights."[41] Abul A'lā Mawdūdī also is inconsistent when he writes of the "irrevocable nature" of the "rights" of non-Muslims, which "cannot be deprived of them unless they renounce the covenant which grants them citizenship." It is no wonder that he interchanges the terms "rights" and "privileges" without distinction.[42]

This ambiguity is also seen in the positions taken on specific aspects of the human rights movement. It is characteristic of Muslim apologetes to assert *both* that modern values are really Islamic in nature and that Islamic values are superior to those advanced today. Illustrative of the former is the argument that the current notion of social security is prefigured in the Qur'ānic injunctions to care for the poor, widows, and orphans, and in the practice of the Prophet and his pious successors. Illustrative of the latter is the idea that Islam provides for a superior system because it covers not only individuals who are disabled or the victims of job accidents but also those who suffer severe family difficulties. Furthermore, the Islamic system is so advanced that the individual need not contribute toward the costs of the benefits provided, for the community as a whole bears the expenses through *zakāt* and special, other taxes.[43] This two-track approach is also found in thinking on democracy. On the one hand there is the thought that parliamentary democracy is really Islamic because of God's command of consultation and because of the institution of the consultative assembly (*majlis al-shūrā*). On the other hand Islam provides for a more refined version of democracy, since it alone seeks to realize morality in political life in addition to the material welfare of its people.[44] Finally, both ways of arguing are found in the evaluation of the human rights covenants themselves. One argument holds that these legal texts were anticipated in the Magna Carta-like provisions of classical jurisprudence, while another suggests that Islam is actually superior in the law of human rights because, unlike the international community today, it can enforce its code.[45]

The apologetic approach is seen most clearly in the current Muslim discussion on women's rights. Sa'īd Ramaḍān, for example, argues that the notion of complete equality is found in the Qur'ān and that, in fact, Islam first endowed women with full rights. The lot of Muslim women since the beginning of the Islamic era, he contends, has been far better than that of Western women in the same period.[46] Saudi scholars similarly stress that it was Islam that raised women from their base rank in pre-Islamic Arabia, under Roman law, and during the Christian Middle Ages to the highest position of society. Islam was not only precocious, it is also superior in that it accounts for the stability of the family and the physical weaknesses of women by making certain obligations inapplicable to them (*dūn al-ināth*). Women, then, are spared the same responsibilities of inheritance, testimony, and marriage that are incumbent on men.[47]

155

Like their general positions, these particular arguments of the apologetes ring hollow. They would have us believe, for instance, that the Qur'an in Sura II provides for equality of rights for husband and wife, but the appropriate verse only says that women are to be treated in a "similar" (*mishulu*) manner and makes clear that men have "rank" (*daraja*) over them. They point to the Prophet's solicitude for the women in Anjasha's caravan, the entrusting of the Qur'ān to Hafsa's care, and the example of the pious Rābi'a, to demonstrate the importance of women.[48] Gibb has spoken for most of us in retorting: "When Amīr Ali exclaims: 'Who has not heard of the saintly Râbi'a and a thousand others her equals?' I wonder how many Muslim readers have asked themselves to name even five of those thousand others."[49]

The apologetes are equally unconvincing in their defense of the Islamic position on freedom of religion. To argue that the prohibition on change of religion arose because of Jewish intrigues in al-Madīna in the seventh century[50] is to obscure a cardinal point of Islamic theory--apostasy is both an affront to Allāh and an attack on the political community. It is also to ignore that the apostasy in the Arabian peninsula after Muḥammad's death was the inevitable consequence of the tribal habit of owing allegiance to one leader and of the unfamiliarity of attachment to a transpersonal cause. Although the status of *dhimmīs* is rarely discussed these days, since the great majority of Islamic states do not distinguish among Muslim and non-Muslim citizens, some feel the need to defend the classical notion. For instance, Mawdūdī does so by going on the offensive. In arguing that "nobody can deny the fact that the minorities are almost everywhere deprived of even their basic human rights in the so-called modern national states," he assumes too much. In suggesting that non-Islam-

156

ic states "generally" strip minorities of their identity, engage in genocide, and create caste systems,[51] he generalizes from an exaggerated estimation of the plight of Indian Muslims. Rather than persuading the non-Muslim reader of the inherent humaneness of Islamic policy toward the protected unbelievers, such a manner of argument only induces him to question the reasonableness of the argument.

Conclusion

Edward Said cautions Western students of Islam of what results from a conceptual determinism born of their own cultural values and preferences: "When you can make countries such as Iran or Lebanon seem to fit your ideas of what they are, then you will one day inevitably stand aggressively against intransigent native realities."[52] The warning is apt; so too is his suggestion that a monolithic label like Islam hides a diversity of facts. They are equally relevant, I would suggest, to Muslims themselves who, in presuming to defend the Islamic approach to human rights, often impose their own self-gratifying interpretations on "native realities." To my mind, these latter represent as great a problem as the former, for in their self-deception they misrepresent the Islamic heritage as surely as have Said's Orientalists.

Islam deserves better. It is a great civilization, which preaches respect for life and property, which practices tolerance and fraternity. Abhorring infanticide and tribal feuding, espousing the protection of women and the needy, and urging the creation of a just social and economic order, Islam unquestionably shares much of the spirit of the present human rights movement. In these days when Islamic fundamentalists are branded fanatical, xenophobic, and anti-Semitic, we will do well to remember Islam's justified reputation for openness in the European "Dark Ages." Even the venerable Abelard testified to the attractiveness of Saracen forebearance of non-Muslims. Distraught from ecclesiastical pressures and conciliar judgments, he admitted in his *Historia calamitatum*: "I fell into such a state of despair that I thought of quitting the realm of Christendom and going over to the heathen, there to live a quiet Christian life amongst the enemies of Christ at the cost of what tribute was asked."[53]

The contributions of Islam to respect for the individual, however, do not negate the fact that there are differences with the prevailing notion of human rights. Islam does not advance the basic idea of inalienable rights, nor does it avoid distinguishing according to sex and religion, as Article 2 of the Universal Declaration enjoins, nor does it allow change of religion, as Article 18 of the declaration provides. I wish to be clear that these differences do not make Islam inferior or out of touch with the modern world. To the contrary, they remind us that there are multiple valid approaches to the realization of man's dignity. It is a particularly useful reminder in an era in which diplomats and international lawyers would have us believe that human rights are not subject to cultural variations. The case of Islam is sufficient to make the point that the current legal covenants incorporate "rights" that are not universally acceptable.

Yet it is obvious that a great many Muslims feel as if Islam suffers by comparison to these international documents and so feel it necessary to defend it. In doing so, apologetes take liberties and make distortions that render our understanding of Islam as an alternative approach even more elusive. Asserting that Islam has a

full-blown concept of the "rights of man" and in-
sisting that women receive equal treatment serve
no purpose other than to console their authors.
Smith described the phenomenon well:

> The more acutely is felt the inadequacy of one's
> present, the more one insists on the splendour
> of one's past. In the Muslim case, the crucial-
> ly important religious factor is added. For
> those dubious of Islam as a sufficient or effec-
> tive ideal today of the good life in community,
> the endeavour is pushed hard to show that in the
> past it was spectacularly so. The more insecure
> one's faith, the more imperious the drive to
> argue for this. It becomes seemingly indispen-
> sable to one's relation both to the modern world
> and to eternal destiny that this conclusion be
> maintained--and even that any adverse evidence
> be repressed.[54]

The demands of modernization have only intensified this tendency among Muslims. Both the traditionalists and the modernists, the Saudis and
Iraqis for instance, face the same dilemma: how to
acquire the benefits of advanced technology and
social organization without abandoning the traditional values of the people. In struggling with
this cruel predicament, both--and not merely the
modernists, as Gibb and Smith thought--have adopted
Western symbols and forms to justify Islam's
progressive nature. Several adverse consequences
ensue.

One is the historical distortion of Islam itself, which results from the determination to find
good, liberal values in the classical sources. It
is a dangerous practice, however, for like the
work of the Mu'tazila, it challenges the transcen-
dentalism of Islam by introducing an alien utili-
tarianism, and like the sin of the *ahl al-shirk*,

159

it introduces new deities alongside Allāh.[55] Seyyed Hossein Nasr has made the point succinctly: "Some modernized Muslims, who instead of wanting to make men God-like wish to make God man-like, especially like twentieth century man, have tried simply to equate *ijmā'* with parliamentary 'democracy'."[56] This tendency debilitates the traditionalists and modernists wondering where to move by obscuring whence they came.

A second consequence of the facile identification of Western and Islamic values is the inducement of unwarranted complacency, often precluding careful judgments. The assertion that women are not unequal in Islam is reassuring, but it is not the answer to the hard question, for the traditionalists, of whether modifications must be adopted, and for the modernists, of whether traditional practices must be retained. To assume equality is, for the traditionalists, to accept largely that changes are not necessary, and for the modernists, to believe that most changes are acceptable. In either case it is to abnegate the responsibility that would flow from a balanced description of Islamic theory like the following: "From the Islamic point of view the question of equality of men and women is meaningless. It is like discussing the equality of a rose and jasmine....Each has certain duties and functions in accordance with his or her nature and constitution."[57] Prudent leaders accepting this statement would need continually to rethink how their society might satisfy sexual complementarity in changing circumstances. A general example of the intellectual self-satisfaction that results from proposing that Islam and "modern" values are entirely compatible is the shah of Iran's overlooking the depth of traditionalist objections to his modernizing vision.

A final consequence of apologetics is the stimu-

lation of Western disbelief and criticism. React-
ing to the perception of infidel attack on Islam,
the apologetes have crafted defenses that belie adherence to the canons of historiographical objec-
tivity (which, I hasten to add, are infrequently
met elsewhere as well). All too often the Western
reader, asked to believe that social security is
an Islamic creation or that Magna Carta was but an
imperfect facsimile of the developed Islamic idea
of civil liberties, has responded by dismissing
the seriousness of contemporary Islamic thought.
The result will be the perpetuation of Western
stereotypes of Islam, and the excitement of greater
defensiveness and resentment among Muslims. While
the problem of perception is surely two-sided, and
while Westerners themselves indisputably indulge
in their own apologetics, Muslim writers would do
well to disappoint the smug expectations of their
would-be critics.

Whatever the future of apologetics, it is clear
that the Islamic world is in a period of upheaval
and change, when the reconciliation of Islam and
modernization is uncertain for both traditionalists
and modernists. Perhaps, as Professor Khadduri
said in 1946, "the parochial traditions can be
gradually modified by developing new traditions influenced by the new ideas,"[58] but for the moment
the parochial traditions, the new traditions, and
the new ideas coexist uncomfortably. The recent
events in Iran are only the latest demonstration of
the persistence of the traditional faith as one of
the fundamental pillars of the modern Muslim's
life; the inability of the Egyptian Government to
pass a law of personal status and the Islamic references in the constitution of the Marxist People's Democratic Republic of Yemen provide other
evidence of the tenacity of Islam in even the "revolutionary" states. Out of every country where
there are believers, then, issues the Islamic

161

challenge: to Muslims to be true to their heritage
in responding to the attractiveness of the human
rights ideal, and to proponents of that ideal to
ponder the universality of their declarations and
covenants.

Notes

1. Qur'ān, 17:70. The same verse also says that man has been given preference (*faḍḍalunāhumu*) in the order of Creation.

2. See Section 169 of *La Chanson de Roland* in *A Survey of French Literature*, ed. Morris Bishop (New York: Harcourt, Brace & World, 1965), p. 11. See also chapter 11 of *Candide* in *Three Philosophical Voyages* (New York: Dell, 1964), p. 115.

3. From his *Jamharat ansāb al-'Arab*, quoted in *Race and Color in Islam*, by Bernard Lewis (New York: Harper & Row, 1971), p. 21

4. See, for example, Saïd Ramadan, *Islam: Doctrine et mode de vie*, no. 3 (Geneva: Centre Islamique, Dhul Qa'dah 1380/May, 1961), pp. 8-10.

5. See Walter Ulmann, *Medieval Papalism: The Political Theories of the Medieval Canonists* (London: Methuen, 1949), p. 122.

6. Lewis, pp. 19-22.

7. The phrase is Eric Voegelin's--who, curiously, does not address himself to the "transcendental irruption" of Islam. *Order and History*, vol. II, *The World of the Polis* (Baton Rouge, La.: Louisiana State University Press, 1957), p. 1.

8. Qur'ān, 17:31.

9. Ibid., 4:3; 2:225; 2:178.

10. Ibid., 2:29.

11. Joseph Schacht, *An Introduction to Islamic Law* (Oxford: The Clarendon Press, 1964), pp. 113, 176.

12. Qur'ān, 4:13, 14, 59, 69, 80.

13. N.J. Coulson finds it significant that "no adequate machinery...is provided by the legal theory

to protect the individual against the state." "The State and the Individual in Islamic Law," *The International and Comparative Law Quarterly*, 6, pt. 1 (January, 1957), p. 59.

14. Qur'ān, 4:34.

15. Ibid., 60:10.

16. Ibid., 2:228-32.

17. Ibid., 4:11, 176.

18. Ibid., 67:25.

19. Cited by Majid Khadduri, *War and Peace in the Law of Islam* (Baltimore: The Johns Hopkins University Press, 1955), p. 150.

20. Ibid., pp. 76-77.

21. Qur'ān, 2:221.

22. Ibid., 9:5.

23. Khadduri, pp. 177, 195-98.

24. Mohammad Talaat al-Ghunaimi, *The Muslim Conception of International Law and the Western Approach* (The Hague: Martinus Nijhoff, 1968), pp. 82, 151, 186-87.

25. Qur'ān, 2:178.

26. Ibid., 5:41.

27. Ibid., 24:2-5.

28. The assassin of King Faysal, a prince of the royal family, was beheaded in June, 1975. Princess Mashal bint 'Abd al-'Azīz was executed for illegal intercourse in mid-1977. See *Times* (London), 1 February 1978, p. 6. For information on the British citizens see *Times* (London), 17 June 1978, pp. 4, 13.

29. For background information see David Bonderman, "Modernization and Changing Perceptions of

Islamic Law," *Harvard Law Review*, 81, no. 6 (April, 1968): 1169-93; J.N.D. Anderson, "Modern Trends in Islam: Legal Reform and Modernization in the Middle East," *The International and Comparative Law Quarterly*, 20, pt. 1 (January, 1971), pp. 1-21.

30. See Norman Anderson, *Law Reform in the Muslim World* (London: The Athlone Press, 1976), pp. 100-62.

31. United Nations, General Assembly, *Official Records*, 3d sess, Third Committee (Lake Success, New York: 21 September-8 December 1948), pp. 391-92, 403-405. (Hereafter, comparable U.N. citations will begin with *Official Records*.)

32. *Official Records*, 9th sess., Third Committee (New York: 22 September-15 December 1954), pp. 116-117, 145-46; *Official Records*, 15th sess., Third Committee (New York: 21 September-16 December 1960), pp. 197-98, 202-203, 206, 214, 222-23, quote at 214.

33. *Official Records*, 3d sess. (1948), Third Committee, p. 515; *Official Records*, 11th sess., Third Committee (New York: 12 November 1956-12 February 1957), p. 238. For a general discussion of "social security," *takāful ijtimā'ī*, in Islam, see 'Alī 'Alī Manṣūr, *Nuẓum al-ḥukm wa al-idāra* (Beirut: Dār al-fataḥ liltibā'a wa al-nashr, 1391/1971).

34. *Official Records*, 16th sess., Third Committee (New York: 20 September-14 December 1961), p. 153.

35. *Official Records*, 3d sess. (1948), Third Committee, pp. 363-65, 367-70.

36. *Official Records*, 30th sess., Third Committee (17 September-5 December 1975), p. 365.

37. See Wilfred Cantwell Smith, *Islam in Modern History* (Princeton: Princeton University Press, 1957), pp. 115-55. See also H.A.R. Gibb, *Modern Trends in Islam* (Chicago: The University of Chicago Press, 1947), pp. 106-29.

38. A.K. Hubaiti, "Human Rights in Islam," *The Journal Rabetat al-'Alām al-Islami*, 4, no. 5 (Rabi' ul-Aluwal 1397/March, 1977), pp. 61-62.

39. Muḥammad Khalaf Allāh Aḥmad, "Mawqif al-haḍāra al-islāmiyya min ḥaqūq al-insān," *Revue Egyptienne de droit international*, 12, Book 2 (1956, 2d semester), pp. 1-21.

40. Khalid M. Ishaque, "Human Rights in Islamic Law," *The Review, International Commission of Jurists*, no. 12 (June, 1944), pp. 31-39.

41. Al-Ghunaimi, pp. 215-16, 189.

42. Abul A'la Mawdudi, *Human Rights in Islam* (Leicester: The Islamic Foundation, 1396/1976), pp. 10, 11.

43. Ahmed Zaki Yamani, *Islamic Law and Contemporary Issues* (Jidda: The Saudi Publishing House, Rajab 1388), pp. 42-47.

44. Abdul Qader Audah, *Islam: Between Ignorant Followers and Incapable Scholars* (Salmiyah: International Islamic Federation of Student Organizations, 1391/1971), pp. 59, 66-67, 73, 91, 99; Mawdudi, p. 8. For latter line of thought see also Mahmoud F. Hoballah, *Islam and Modern Values* (Washington, D.C.: The Islamic Center, n.d.), p. 9.

45. Mawdudi, pp. 13-14. See also *Nadwat 'ilimiyyat hawla al-Sharīat al-Islamiyyat wa ḥaqūq al-insān fī al-islām* (Beirut: Dār al-kitāb al-lubnānī, 1973), pp. 111, 116, 94.

46. Saïd Ramadan, *Trois grands problèmes de l'Islam dans le monde contemporain* (Geneva: Centre islamique, Rajab 1380/January, 1961), pp. 7-13.

47. *Nadwat 'ilimiyyat*, pp. 134-38, 141.

48. Abdullah Yusuf Ali translated the particular verse of Sūra II as: "And women shall have rights/ Similar to the rights/Against them, according/To

166

what is equitable;/But men have a degree (of advantage) over them." But he went on to offer the following interpretation: "The difference in economic position between the sexes makes the man's rights and liabilities a little greater than the woman's. Q.iv.34 refers to the duty of the man to maintain the woman, and to a certain difference in nature between the sexes. *Subject to this, the sexes are on terms of equality in law,* and in certain matters the weaker sex is entitled to special protection" (emphasis added). See *The Holy Qur-an, Text, Translation and Commentary,* vol. I (New York: Hafner, 1946), p. 90. See also Ramadan, pp. 9-10.

49. Gibb, p. 108.

50. *Nadwat 'ilimiyyat,* p. 38.

51. Abul A'lā Maudūdī, *Rights of Non-Muslims in Islamic States* (Lahore: Islamic Publications, Ltd., 1961), pp. 4-5.

52. Edward W. Said, "Whose Islam?" *New York Times,* 29 January 1979, p. A 17.

53. *Historia calamitatum* in *The Letters of Abelard and Heloise,* trans. Betty Radice (Middlesex: Penguin, 1974), p. 94.

54. Smith, pp. 117-18.

55. See Gibb, p. 120.

56. Seyyed Hossein Nasr, *Ideals and Realities of Islam* (London: George Allen & Unwin, 1966), p. 100.

57. Ibid., p. 112.

58. Majid Khadduri, "Human Rights in Islam," *Annals of the American Academy of Political and Social Science,* 243 (1946): 81.

HUMAN RIGHTS IN LATIN AMERICAN POLITICAL CULTURE: THE ROLE OF THE CHURCHES

BRIAN H. SMITH

Over the past fifteen years the military have seized power in most major South American countries, leaving only Colombia and Venezuela with democratic regimes. The armed forces claim that only they are capable of controlling the domestic violence and social disruptions that accompanied the rapid political and economic changes of the 1960's. This process of social conflict and subsequent military intervention has been especially notable in the countries of the subcontinent region--Brazil, Bolivia, Chile, Argentina, Peru, and Uruguay.

Military rule, however, has not led to a decline in violence; indeed, most of these governments have resorted to extremely repressive measures in pursuing their objectives. In responding to the problems that brought them to power (labor unrest, inflation, societal polarization, and the growth of Marxist parties or guerrilla movements), the mili-

"Churches and Human Rights in Latin America: Recent Trends in the Subcontinent" (under which title this essay was first published) by Brian H. Smith is reprinted from Journal of Interamerican Studies and World Affairs, *Vol. 21, No. 1 (February, 1979), pp. 89-127, by permission of the publisher, Sage Publications, Inc.*

tary have employed severe measures to restore order and promote more stable economic growth. These efforts have involved placing strict controls on organized labor, student groups, and political parties, suspending constitutional guarantees and processes, and offering generous incentives to domestic producers and foreign investors. Power has been consolidated by effective mobilization of the forces of physical coercion (the armed forces and the police) and by the appeal to traditional emotion-laden symbols such as anticommunism, nationalism, and protection of private property.[1] Although guerrilla activity has declined and inflation rates have slowed in some places, these military regimes, in the process of promoting stability, have systematically violated a whole gamut of human rights as guaranteed by the two United Nations covenants--the International Covenant on Civil and Political Rights and the International Covenant on Economic, Social, and Cultural Rights.[2]

Amidst this atmosphere of repression, churches have become important actors in the struggle to counter these abuses of state power in the subcontinent. At the international level, church networks have become one of the most reliable sources of information to the outside world on the extent of rights violations inside these countries. In turn the international network of the churches has provided considerable financial and material support to groups working to defend and promote human rights in the southern tier of Latin America.

At the national level, the Catholic bishops of these Latin churches have increased their public condemnations of abuses of power. In so doing, they not only have denounced such crimes as murder, torture, and denial of habeas corpus and fair trial, but also have pointed to what they believe are the deeper underlying causes precipitating the rapid increase of such systematic violations of human rights--unjust economic structures, maldistribution of land and wealth, lack of effective social participation by the poor, and the pervasiveness of an ideology of national security that subjugates all rights of the person to the expediency of the state.[3]

Several of the most recent pastoral letters of the bishops of Brazil, Chile, and Argentina, for example, have clearly emphasized that there is a connection between violation of classic civil rights and the desire upon the part of wealthy elites to preserve their economic power. They point to a clear relationship between abuse of persons (especially the poor) and a refusal to respect basic economic and social rights in society by those who benefit from military rule.[4] They also call upon existing governments as well as landed and industrial elites to make profound changes in the economic and social systems as a necessary step to guarantee the full panoply of human rights as defined by the international covenants of the United Nations.

Most of these episcopal letters have urged secular leaders to make such changes as greater distribution of land and other economic resources, respect for independent labor unions, effective social participation by the poor in decisions affecting their lives, and fair application of law to limit government power. In these documents the bishops also commit the organizational network of the Church to a vigorous defense of those whose rights are being violated and to a more profound identification with the plight of the poor.[5] This general concern for human rights and new commitment to the oppressed have legitimized the setting up of a whole new series of social and pastoral programs in Latin American churches over the past decade, including the new Church-sponsored organizations concerned with the promotion of human rights. Since the early 1970's churches in Chile, Brazil, Paraguay, Bolivia, and Argentina[6] have created new religious and social structures to respond to the needs of the poor who have borne the brunt of repression in these respective countries.

While the documents of the hierarchies in these countries have been widely publicized in South America as well as in Western Europe and North America, to date there has been little research done on these newly emerging human rights commissions and lay leadership programs functioning at lower levels of the churches. The activities of these new organizations have expanded rapidly in the last several years, and they not only have provided substantial assistance to those suffering human rights violations but have also precipitated serious conflict between Church and state and, at times, tension within the respective churches themselves.

It is therefore important to study these new organizations in greater detail in order to assess the Church's real capacity to promote the structural changes the bishops see as a necessary basis for the observance of all human rights. Such information is also important to assess what contradictions are emerging for churches as a whole in this work and whether they can continue to make an active promotion of human rights an essential part of their religious mission.

This paper will focus on the learning experiences and accomplishments of Church-sponsored human rights commissions and other pastoral programs that have emerged since the early 1970's in Chile, Brazil, Paraguay, Bolivia, and Argentina. I shall analyze (1) under what conditions, and with what type of support, these programs have emerged, (2) what range of activities they have undertaken to promote civil, political, social, and economic rights, and (3) what impact they have had on both the political system and the respective national churches themselves.

I shall give brief descriptive overviews of the activities of each of these churches in the area of human rights using the three questions above as organizing components for the available empirical data. In a concluding section I will offer a comparative analysis of all five cases as to what they reveal regarding the capacities and limitations of churches as complex organizations in protecting and promoting the full gamut of human rights.

I. Chile: The Committee of Cooperation for Peace, the Vicariate of Solidarity, and the Base Communities

Within three weeks of Chile's military coup of September 11, 1973, Catholic, Protestant, and Jewish leaders moved to establish emergency committees to assist refugees and also families of those who had been killed or jailed or who had disappeared. There are several reasons why church leaders acted so quickly and with government acquiescence. In previous years all church leaders had been forced to take the social concerns of the poor more seriously due to the steady movement to the left in the political system since the early 1960's. During both Frei's and Allende's presidencies many church groups focused more efforts on identifying with problems of the poor, and the Catholics had begun to establish small basic communities in working-class areas to evangelize the poor more effectively. The churches also maintained fairly cordial relations with the Marxist government and established closer communication with one another in the process. When the coup occurred, by and large major church leaders publicly remained neutral. The Permanent Committee of the Catholic Conference even issued a mildly critical declaration two days after the coup, lamenting the bloodshed and calling upon the military to respect all gains made by the working classes during the last decade.[7]

In the aftermath of the coup, when thousands were being tortured, murdered, or put in large concentration camps, the persecuted turned in droves to the churches for help. All other major social and political organizations were placed under strict controls, and the past performance, current neutrality, and existing organizational network of the churches (especially the Catholic Church) made them ready channels of assistance. Furthermore, the particularly brutal nature of the repression shocked international public opinion, and Protestant and Catholic Church groups in Western Europe and North America were most willing to provide immediate financial and material assistance to Chilean church leaders attempting to help those in need. The new military regime acquiesced reluctantly to church efforts to assist those being persecuted, seeking religious legitimation for having overturned the longstanding democratic traditions of the country, and because it had no effective mechanism to handle the human casualties of its own brutality.

Finally, due to the long and vigorous history of political participation and multiparty competition in the country, many civilian leaders were anxious and willing to do something to counter the repression and assist those being persecuted. Many, especially in parties associated with the Christian Left--MAPU and "Izquierda Cristiana"--had formerly been active in church-sponsored educational or social programs in the 1960's and found no difficulty in moving back into church structures to carry out humanitarian programs.

All of these political and religious factors in the context of sudden and brutal repression led to the formation of the Committee of Cooperation for Peace by seven major religious denominations in the country.[8] Over the next two years the committee established a whole range of services for Chileans suffering the effects of the coup--legal aid, assistance to workers arbitrarily dismissed from their jobs, medical programs in areas where public health clinics had been suspended, small self-help projects for the unemployed, and soup kitchens in urban working-class areas for starving children. The committee also established regional offices in fifteen of the twenty-five provinces where similar projects were begun. By 1975 over three hundred full-time lawyers, social workers, and medical personnel were working in various parts of the country, and the annual budget (over $2 million) was provided mainly by Protestant and Catholic sources in North America and Western Europe and some nonconfessional agencies.[9]

In December, 1975, General Pinochet demanded the churches disband the Committee for Peace for having assisted many Chileans sought by the secret police (DINA) to leave the country. The government also argued that many civilians formerly associated with the Allende government were using the committee to continue their political activities under church auspices. Thus, under severe pressure from both Pinochet and the government-controlled press, church leaders agreed to close the committee in late December. However, Cardinal Silva immediately moved to incorporate many of the activities and personnel of the former Committee for Peace into a new organization under Catholic auspices--the Vicariate of Solidarity--established in late January, 1976. Over the past two years this Vicariate has established offices in the majority of Chile's twenty-five dioceses. These offices provide legal and

health services, manage between forty and fifty
farm cooperatives in rural areas, and support soup
kitchens for hungry children and adults in major
urban areas. The Vicariate also issues a biweekly
bulletin (*Solidaridad*) from its Santiago headquarters that publishes accounts of its various
projects as well as data on malnutrition, unemployment, and disappeared persons. Its budget is somewhat larger than that of the Committee for Peace,
though funds are drawn mainly from the same foreign
sources as supported that group. The Protestant
churches have also continued to support, on their
own, self-help worker enterprises with assistance
from Western European sources.[10]

In addition to the work of the Committee for
Peace and its successor, the Vicariate, the small
base communities established in most of the twenty-
five Catholic dioceses of the country have taken on
new vitality and importance since the coup. During
the Frei and Allende years these groups did not at-
tract significant numbers of people, due to the expanding activities of social and political organizations associated with parties. But since 1973
these neighborhood groups have become the only
opportunities for Chileans (especially in working-
class areas) to meet and discuss their problems.
These communities are subdivided into three or four
sectors, each focusing on different religious or
social issues--Bible study, catechetical training,
prayer, and self-help social services. Thus far
there has been no systematic study of these groups,
but it was estimated in 1975 that there were approximately twenty thousand active leaders of these
communities and ten thousand more (almost exclusively women) who had received extensive training as
catechists.[11]

Taken together, the activities of all of these
programs and structures operating under Church

auspices in contemporary Chile have dealt with the effects of violations of a broad range of civil, social, and economic rights. So far their impact on changing the political and economic structures that cause such violations has, however, been minimal. Official repression continues, with almost no opportunity for effective participation or distribution of resources in favor of the poor. In fact, the policies of the junta have rolled back most of the working-class gains made under Frei and Allende--labor unions are under government surveillance, wages are limited, agrarian reform organizations are being dismantled, and speculators are permitted to amass wealth and buy up enterprises formerly owned by the government. Arrests and tortures have subsided since 1974 and 1975, but the courts only very recently have begun to act with any independence and accept the Vicariate's legal requests to investigate lists of disappeared persons.

Despite their inability to affect direct change, the work of the Committee for Peace and the Vicariate have had an impact in other important ways. These committees have amassed well-documented evidence on civil rights violations. Based upon these reports and other sources (e.g., early on-site inspections and some newspaper stories in Chile), international organizations have been able to publicize continuing rights violations in the country. The Committee for Peace and the Vicariate have also provided survival assistance to thousands who would have perished or despaired, and thus have kept alive a spirit of hope. In addition, the small base communities have nourished a sense of solidarity and critical awareness among working classes, while serving as surrogate training grounds for future political leaders if and when the military relinquishes control of the country.

The impact of these activities on the Church has been considerable, but also not without tensions for the Church itself. For the first time in its history the Chilean Catholic Church is beginning to penetrate the culture of the poor, and urban workers and slum dwellers are identifying with the Church now much more than ever before. But both the upper class and the military are disillusioned with the Church and view it as naive or as an obstacle to their current plans for the country. Right-wing Catholics have also publicly attacked the Church for being infiltrated by Communists.[12] Since the coup nearly two hundred priests (mainly foreigners) have been expelled or urged to leave the country. Criticisms of foreign sources of support for Church programs have also appeared in the press, such as the attempt to discredit the Inter-American Foundation by *El Mercurio* in January, 1978.[13]

Although the hierarchy has occasionally criticized the government for its general economic and political policies, their public documents have been very cautious and usually include some concessions to the government. For example, in their 1975 pastoral letter, "Gospel and Peace," the bishops thanked the military for having saved the country from Marxism and praised the actions of the wives of the military for helping the poor.[14] In their document, "Our Life as a Nation," they said that some abuses of power or unwarranted actions are inevitable and that there is an international campaign to discredit Chile's reputation organized by Marxists abroad.[15] Furthermore, in the four and a half years since the coup, the bishops have seldom criticized the government publicly for torture and have only expressed sharp criticisms (or threatened excommunication) when the authority or person of bishops themselves has been attacked.

This ambiguous stance and selective public criticisms are due to divisions of opinion within the hierarchy as to the merits of the government, to their desire to maintain communication with the military, to an unwillingness to precipitate an all-out war with the state, and to a fear of affecting a more serious public division than already exists among the bishops and faithful alike. As a result, the prophetic role of the bishops has been exercised with extreme caution. But, while at times they have acquiesced to government demands regarding Church-sponsored programs, on the whole their cautious stance has made it possible for the whole new network of human rights activities at lower levels of the Church to continue with some degree of effectiveness, under implicit Church protection.

II. *Brazil: Small Base Communities, Justice and Peace Commissions, and Land Commissions*

The reaction of the churches to the Brazilian military coup of March, 1964, was not as swift or dramatic as in Chile. Moreover, new church structures to promote human rights in Brazil have not been able, so far, to mobilize with the same degree of effectiveness and coordination as in Chile. Nevertheless, some new programs have begun to operate in the past few years affecting civil, social, and economic rights, and small base communities are now mushrooming in many rural areas of the country and perform similar critical roles to those in Chile.

There are many reasons for this relatively slow reaction to an authoritarian regime by the Brazilian Church. First, when the coup occurred, the great majority of the hierarchy acquiesced in hopes that the new government would be able to control the social turmoil of the Goulart administration and carry out its own announced plan for stable and effective economic development.[16] Furthermore, the immediate aftermath of the Brazilian coup was not as brutal and repressive as in Chile. The military did not immediately resort to widespread torture or mass murder, nor did they close Congress and suppress all forms of social participation. In addition, although the Brazilian Church, like the Chilean, had begun to involve itself in social issues in the early 1960's (paralleling the new awakening of social consciousness in the universal Church reflected by Vatican II), neither the hierarchy as a whole nor the laity was strongly committed to this option. A small core of bishops, centering around Dom Helder Camara, were urging a more active social commitment by the Church, but, by 1964, they had lost influence in the National Conference of Brazilian Bishops (CNBB).[17] Many Catholic Action lay leaders active in promoting social change in rural areas in the pre-1964 period moved away from the Church by 1965, when the bishops attempted to exercise stricter controls on their programs and eliminate all activities with political repercussions.[18] Hence, in the aftermath of the coup, the leadership of the CNBB favored cooperation with what seemed to be a moderate regime, and in any case the Church lacked the organizational capacity or network to oppose official policies.

In 1968, however, the government began to impose more repressive measures to curb escalating opposition and eliminate growing leftist guerrilla activities. Habeas corpus was suspended, all civilian control over security forces was eliminated, the Congress, the courts, and the press were severely curtailed, and the use of torture became systematic and widespread. These repressive policies also began to affect the Church itself, as Church publications, radio stations, and pastoral programs in rural areas were placed under close surveillance and some Church personnel (especially in rural areas) harassed, imprisoned, or expelled.[19]

In such an atmosphere of controlled and systematic repression that also touched the institutional church itself, bishops as a group began to criticize the regime, and new Church structures at the local level (base communities and self-help social programs) emerged as alternate forms of social participation and humanitarian assistance for the poor. In May, 1970, the Episcopal Conference published its first major public criticism, denouncing the use of torture and lack of fair trials and expressing the need for greater social participation and respect for legitimate criticism of government policies.[20]

At this time several dioceses began to implement some of the new pastoral orientations of Medellín--formation of small base communities, lay leadership training, and social action favoring the poor. In the northeast of Brazil, for example, where the repressive political and economic policies of the regime have been the most severe (and where harassment of clergy first began), both base communities and social programs run by lay leaders began to take root by the late 1960's.[21] Small base religious communities also sprang up in the early 1970's in the center-west and in several urban areas, such as São Paulo. They emerged in response to the elimination of other forms of social participation. Although these communities are in the beginning stages of development and face problems due to long-standing patterns of personalistic piety, the rootlessness of migrants, and lack of well-trained personnel, they have mushroomed throughout Brazil over the past five years.

No systematic study of these groups has yet been done, but it is estimated that about fifty thousand such centers are operating at present.[22] The Episcopal Conference in 1976 issued a document outlining the focus and purpose of such base communities.

Included in the desired activities of these groups is the development of critical social and political awareness among the participants.[23] The political sensitivity of these orientations has led to increasing numbers of arrests of lay leaders and technical experts assisting these communities, and many have been tortured.[24]

In addition to these new grassroots self-help programs and religious communities, the National Episcopal Conference in 1972 authorized the establishment of Justice and Peace Commissions, both at the national level as part of the CNBB itself and in several dioceses. The purpose of these commissions is to conduct study projects of socio-economic needs of various regions and provide assistance to prisoners and their families. Due to the lack of staff and the weak structural development of the Church in many areas of the country, these commissions have not yet begun to function effectively.

In the archdiocese of São Paulo, however, with the largest concentration of population in the country (over ten million people) and one of the most outspoken of the Brazilian bishops, Cardinal Evaristo Arns, the Justice and Peace Commission over the past few years has inaugurated several programs pertaining to violations of civil, social, and economic rights. In 1975 it published two books on the link between private death squads and security forces in the early days of the government and on the maldistribution of income and economic resources in the archdiocese.[25] Lists of disappeared persons were also printed in the archdiocesan newspaper, *O São Paulo*, based on documented evidence brought to the commission by private individuals and Church personnel. In 1977 the commission received grants from the Inter-American Foundation and from Catholic organizations in West Germany. With some additional local contributions, the commission expanded its personnel to provide emergency relief for prisoners, ex-prisoners, and their families, offer legal and social services to the labor sector, disseminate information on commission activities, and assist other dioceses in the creation of similar commissions.

In addition to Justice and Peace Commissions the bishops of the Amazon region have started programs for Indians and small land-holders who are being displaced by government development projects and large national and international agrobusiness enterprises. Under the auspices of the National Justice and Peace Commission and the CNBB's Commission of Missionary Action, meetings were held in June, 1975, by prelates and technicians in these areas to discuss the dispossession of peasants and to begin legal aid and educational programs to help protect their land claims.[26] Since then, similar programs have been inaugurated by several Amazon dioceses, but--as with the base communities--large numbers of participants have been harassed, arrested, or murdered.

While not as well organized or funded as the Chilean Church's activities for human rights, these new programs in Brazil have attempted to promote and defend a whole range of civil, social, and economic rights of the oppressed. Their impact so far on government and business policy has not been dramatic. While the number of cases of torture and disappearances has decreased since 1974 and the Congress has been reopened and censorship bans have been lifted on several publications, no effective political participation exists for the vast number of citizens. Nor has the government changed its economic strategy of development that allows industrialists and agricultural enterprises to amass great wealth and land at the expense of workers, peasants, and Indians.[27]

As in the Chilean case, one of the most effective
but limited contributions of these new programs has
been the provision of alternate forms of social participation for the poor and powerless. While not
effecting significant changes in economic and political structures, these at least have provided
opportunities for some self-help and for nurturing
a critical awareness and sense of dignity among
them.

The impact of these structures on the Church,
however, has been very notable since 1970, for the
government has increased its surveillance and
harassment of participants in these small base communities, self-help projects, Justice and Peace
Commissions, and land commissions. In addition,
paramilitary death squads and security forces have
murdered several priests, and even kidnapped a
bishop for a short period of time in 1976. More
persecution of Church personnel is occurring in
Brazil than in Chile. This has not only solidified
Church identity with the oppressed but also
stimulated the hierarchy as a group to issue more
decisive denunciations of the government. In this
way the equilibrium of the institutional church is
now clearly on the side of the lower classes.
Thus, in November, 1976, and again in February,
1977, the National Conference of Brazilian Bishops
issued strongly worded documents condemning the
murder of priests and Indians, attacking policies
that absolutize national security, and bluntly
stating that the present model of Brazilian development is characterized by injustice and promotes
institutionalized violence.[28] Both of these documents are far more consistent and critical of the
government than comparable statements by the
Chilean hierarchy. It is also clear that a consensus now exists among higher and lower leaders in

the Brazilian Church that opposition to the government is necessary, since the state itself has singled out the Church for special repression as a subversive organization.[29]

The Church has suffered both external limitation and increasing internal tensions as a result of its human rights programs and the prophetic stance of its bishops. For example, the Church is heavily dependent on the state for maintaining its schools, universities, radio stations, and hospitals, and since the late 1960's the government has curtailed funding for these operations and levied taxes on Church properties. Increasing numbers of foreign priests are being expelled from the country, and the archdiocesan newspaper of Sao Paulo is one of the few remaining newspapers subject to censorship prior to publication. In late 1976 the Church was also ordered to withdraw some of its personnel from mission territories where murder and dispossession of Indians and peasants are occurring, although later the order was reversed.

Right-wing Catholics belonging to the "Tradition, Fatherland and Family" movement also have increased their public attacks on the Church as being infiltrated by Communists. One bishop who belongs to this organization (and who owns a considerable amount of land), Archbishop Geraldo Sigaud of Diamantina, in February, 1977, publicly accused two fellow bishops of being Communists--Bishop Pedro Casaldáliga of São Felix and Bishop Tomáz Balduino of Goias Velho.[30] Both of the accused have been active in defending the land claims of peasants and Indians in rural areas. The government mounted a major public campaign to discredit these two prelates and gave Archbishop Sigaud's accusation widespread circulation in the government-controlled media. Only strong pressure by the Vatican and the Episcopal Conference kept the minister of the interior from expelling Casaldáliga (a Spaniard) from the country. All of these events, however, point to continual Church-state conflicts in the near future and further external pressures by the government to circumscribe human rights activities by Catholic religious and lay leaders.

Unlike the Chilean Church, the Brazilian Church's official concern with human rights originated in a direct attack on the Church itself, and as this attack has intensified so have the efforts of many bishops, priests, and lay leaders to promote civil, social, and economic rights of the poor. The institutional infrastructure of the Brazilian Church and the amount of foreign support for its human rights programs are both far less developed than is the case in Chile. The bishops attempt to offset this institutional weakness through more aggressive public denunciations than the Chilean bishops, but this in turn precipitates stronger official repression of local action programs. The institutional power of the Church to blunt the authoritarian policies of the regime is therefore limited, but as repression continues the whole character of the Church is gradually changing and its mission to the poor more consciously felt and affirmed.

III. *Paraguay: Peasant Leagues, Small Base Communities, and the Committee of Churches for Emergency Assistance*

The oldest continuous dictatorship in South America exists in Paraguay, where Alfredo Stroessner has held power since 1954. In this highly personalistic regime, almost all social institutions in the country (unions, professional associations, courts, universities, business organizations) are controlled or infiltrated by Stroessner sympathizers. A powerful police force (operating under continuous state-of-siege conditions) maintains "order," and the system as a whole is held together by a highly pervasive pattern of corruption supported by profits from institutionalized smuggling.[31]

Between 1958 and 1975 there were five brief but intense waves of arrests and torture involving political opponents of the regime--students, labor leaders, dissident members of the Colorado party (Stroessner's official group), suspected members of a small Communist party. In April and May, 1976, however, a new and more widespread wave of repression occurred aimed particularly at members of the Protestant and Catholic clergy and peasant and Indian leaders associated with church programs, especially in rural areas. Over a thousand men and women were arrested at this time, and many were subjected to torture and other forms of cruel and inhuman treatment in thirteen detention centers in various parts of the country. In addition, thirty-two of Paraguay's thirty-four foreign Jesuit priests were expelled from the country.[32]

Although the government claimed that these programs were supporting guerrillas and planning violent revolution, no substantial proof was provided to justify these claims, nor is there any significant terrorist activity in the country.[33] The real reason for the repression of church personnel was the fact that both Catholic and Protestant church organizations have set up independent structures for both social and religious participation outside government control. In the aftermath of Vatican II (1962-65) and Medellín (1968) the Catholic Church began to concentrate more effort on evangelizing hitherto neglected groups in Paraguay --peasants and Indians in the interior of the country, who constitute two-thirds of the population. Foreign missionaries (especially Spanish Jesuits) have been most active since the mid-1960's in establishing peasant leagues in rural areas, which

187

include credit unions and small agricultural cooperatives. Money for these projects has been provided by foreign Church agencies (such as Catholic
Relief Services in the United States, and Adveniat
and Misereor in West Germany). Some of the activities of these leagues have included teaching
peasants and Indians their legal rights and helping
them pressure the government to apply its own
agrarian reform and labor laws more fairly. Parallel
to these Catholic peasant leagues have been similar
organizations sponsored by the Disciples of Christ
from the U.S. These also provide credit to small
landholders and train peasants in the rudiments of
government and law as these affect their interests.[34]

Such organizations have enabled peasants and Indians to be more aware of their civil and economic
rights under existing law, while stimulating them
to become spokespersons to represent directly their
own interests without reliance upon any of the organizations associated with the government. Even
though most of the leagues purposely chose peasants
publicly known as members of the ruling Colorado
party, the government was most concerned that they
were being trained in independent organizations outside its control. Furthermore, since these cooperatives and credit unions were able to bypass
intermediary agents in marketing their produce,
they were able to receive fairer prices for their
goods. Large landholders and financial and commercial institutions saw their socio-economic
dominance threatened, and therefore actively opposed
these new programs. All of these factors led to the
harsh crackdown of mid-1976, with massive arrests,
torture, and deportations of clergy and laity
active in the leagues.

The reaction of the churches to this repression
has occurred on several fronts. First, small base
communities and deacon training programs for the

laity have taken on new vitality now that the leagues are more circumscribed. These pastoral programs have begun to flourish in almost all major regions in the interior. They involve small groups of forty to fifty people (mostly men) and combine Bible study and catechetical training with frank discussions of agrarian and social problems, such as the legal right of peasants and Indians to seek redress of grievances and form self-help organizations. These new base communities have also been subject to similar harassment by police forces, but lay leaders are determined to continue their activities despite risk to their lives.[35]

The Catholic hierarchy reacted swiftly and strongly to the mid-1976 wave of arrests, which was accompanied by a press campaign charging Communist infiltration in the Church. On June 15, 1976, all eleven Catholic bishops in Paraguay issued a pastoral letter that was read in churches at Sunday Mass. They denounced unequivocally the use of violence and torture to eliminate subversion (even terrorism) and demanded an end to arbitrary procedures, massive arrests, intimidation of entire peasant villages, confiscation of goods, and prolonged holding of people incommunicado. They also emphasized the need for an efficient and respectable judiciary to administer justice fairly.[36] The bishops condemned the government's campaign of defamation and persecution against the Church, emphasizing that only Church leaders can judge what truly conforms to the Gospel. Finally, they affirmed the "inalienable responsibility of the Church in the promotion of activities which are inherent to it," and renewed their "decision to carry them forward at whatever cost in terms of sacrifice."[37]

The third and final effort to promote and defend human rights by churches in the aftermath of the most recent wave of repression has been the formation of the Committee of Churches for Emergency Assistance. On June 28, 1976, representatives of the Catholic and Lutheran churches and the Disciples of Christ announced the establishment of a new ecumenical organization to help prisoners and their families.[38] The committee operates out of the chancery office of the Episcopal Conference of Paraguay and provides food and medicines to prisoners, economic and rehabilitation assistance to families of prisoners, ex-prisoners, or the disappeared, runs a documentation and information service, and offers legal aid to those charged with crimes.[39] The committee has received financial and material support from the World Council of Churches, Catholic Relief Services (U.S.), Misereor (West Germany), Christian Aid (England), Christian Church (U.S.), and the Catholic Justice and Peace Commission in Holland. Catholic and Protestant leaders in human rights working in other parts of Latin America, North America, and Western Europe have also visited the committee on several occasions over the past two years to give it moral support and international visibility.[40]

The committee has achieved some important results over the past two years. It has been given daily visiting rights to Emboscada prison (where most of the prisoners are now incarcerated), and the living conditions there have improved significantly due to food and medicines the committee has brought in. Literacy training programs and artisan cooperatives have been set up in the prison under the committee's direction. The sale of artisan products such as woodcarvings and woven baskets serves not only to raise additional relief funds but also to circulate public reminders in society at large that there are people in prison.

Lists of prisoners also have been prepared and presented to the International League of Human

Rights during its two visits to Paraguay, in 1976 and 1977. The government has allowed 45 of these prisoners to be processed in civilian courts, and the committee has provided lawyers for the defense of 40 of them. The government has also released over 200 prisoners since September, 1976, so that by December, 1977, there were only 179 remaining in Emboscada. (The whereabouts of many who have disappeared, however, is still not known, and many people are now imprisoned for shorter periods, thus maintaining a climate of fear.) The bulk of the committee's budget (more than half of its funds) is spent on relief programs for families of prisoners or persons who have disappeared in the countryside. To date 177 projects (assisting 224 families) have been set up. These include not only food and clothing but also help to establish or continue self-help projects in farming, artisan work, or husbandry.[41]

In this way the work of the new ecumenical committee has contributed to some significant changes on behalf of legal rights and care of prisoners and survival aid for their families. Furthermore, self-help projects similar to cooperatives begun by Catholic and Protestant churches ten years ago are being reformed with aid from this committee. But the basic structures of political and economic power of the country have not changed significantly. Stroessner is still in complete control and in early February, 1978, was given yet another term in office in a controlled election. The economy has been bolstered by recent financial agreements allowing both Brazil and Argentina to build hydroelectric dams in Paraguayan territory,[42] and no major changes have occurred in the concentration of land and wealth in the country.

The government has made concessions by releasing some prisoners, allowing civil trials for others,

191

and permitting various social and economic improvement programs by the Committee of Churches. These concessions, however, have been due not only to Church denunciations but, more important, to pressure from various international human rights organizations and from the U.S. Government, to which General Stroessner is particularly sensitive. There is no major internal threat to Stroessner's power at present, and he can afford, under prodding by Washington, Amnesty International, and the International League of Human Rights, to loosen the repression a bit in order to maintain U.S. economic and military aid.[43]

Both the peasant leagues and the small base communities, which have been badly crippled but still function, and the Committee of Churches (moving cautiously but swiftly with strong international support during this latest period of decompression) have all had much greater impact on the churches themselves than on the political and economic system. Church leaders and personnel now sense the impact of the repressive nature of the Stroessner regime more than in previous periods, since the most recent attacks have been directed primarily at their own institutions and at clerical and lay personnel. The Catholic hierarchy has clearly committed itself to continue these new social and religious programs as integral parts of the mission of the Church, and in so doing are making the institution more credible than before in the eyes of the vast majority of poor in the country.

The peasant leagues and cooperatives may be smashed, and this fate could also await the new Committee of Churches if Stroessner feels it is getting out of hand and when the recent focus of international attention on Paraguay subsides. The small base communities, Bible study groups, and catechetical and deacon training programs, however, will probably be defended more vigorously by the churches, since they are easier to justify on specifically religious grounds--and also receive very little foreign financial support compared to the other social projects. As in Chile and Brazil, these small groups are breeding grounds for future local leaders who learn to exercise their rights of social participation in surrogate fashion under Church auspices. The sense of dignity and critical awareness of poor people is being kept alive, and in the long run this is far more deleterious to Stroesser's totalitarian regime than food, clothing, medicines, or legal aid programs sponsored by foreigners.

IV. *Bolivia: Justice and Peace Commission and Permanent Assembly of Human Rights*

Official Church opposition to the military regime in Bolivia since 1971, as in the case of Brazil, has been slow in developing. In many ways religious opposition to the Bolivian Government is similar to the Chilean case, where far more significant action on behalf of human rights has occurred at lower levels of the Church and in an ecumenical context.

When General Hugo Banzer overthrew the populist-leftist military government of General Juan José Torres in August, 1971, the Catholic bishops accepted the new regime with relative calm. They lamented the killing, arrests, and deportations that occurred, but expressed hope that the new government would restore order and affirmed that Church buildings were rightful places of asylum for politically persecuted persons.[44] But throughout 1972 the military did not respect this ancient right of asylum in churches, and on several occasions houses of bishops, priests, and nuns were searched and people there seeking help were arrested. In addition, eighteen foreign priests and three Protestant pastors were expelled from the country. Several bishops on their own expressed public criticism of the government for raiding Church buildings, but the twenty-two-man Episcopal Conference (half of whom are foreigners themselves)[45] said nothing.

Although political parties, labor unions, and the press were not as severely repressed in Bolivia in the immediate aftermath of the coup as they were in Chile, during 1972 there were countless numbers of arrests (especially in mining, working-class, and union organizations), and torture and detentions without charge were widespread. After a Jesuit priest was arrested in January, 1973, a public letter was signed by ninety-nine priests, nuns, and Protestant pastors strongly attacking the government for these abuses of power, and also criticizing the Catholic hierarchy for their silence as a group in regard to these violations.[46] At about the same time, a group of Catholic laity and priests convinced the bishops to set up a Justice and Peace Commission (similar to the one begun in Brazil in 1972). This organization was endorsed by the Bolivian Episcopal Conference but not constituted as an official organ of the Church. Rather, it was to be primarily the work of the laity. Dr. Luis Aldolfo Salinas, the last civilian to hold the office of president of the country, in 1969, was named its first president.[47]

Although originally established primarily as a reflection group to study social and economic questions in the light of the Church's social teachings, this group quickly moved into human rights work as a result of popular needs and pressures. It was soon inundated with petitions for legal aid by families seeking the whereabouts of kin who had been arrested or had disappeared. As a result, over the next two years the Justice and Peace Commission expanded its activities to include habeas corpus petitions to the courts for missing persons and material relief for their families. It also established offices in five regions outside La Paz and received financial assistance from Church-sponsored organizations in the U.S. and Western Europe. In turn it became the most reliable source of information on violations occurring within Bolivia upon which international human rights groups (such as Amnesty International) have based their reports.

It also engaged in still other activities affecting sensitive political issues embarrassing to the government. It published over three hundred articles in the press on human rights and pressured the government to issue a general amnesty for political prisoners. Public prayer vigils and fasts in criticism of government policies were also organized.[48] Furthermore, in February, 1975, the commission published a book recounting a massacre of one hundred peasants near Cochabamba perpetrated by the military one year before.

This occurred three months after a major new wave of repression. In November, 1974, the government issued a decree outlawing all public political activities and strikes, placing parties in recess, removing current leaders of all labor, professional, and student organizations, postponing elections scheduled for 1975, and imposing mandatory public service on all citizens over twenty-one years of age. In the face of this repression the Justice and Peace Commission stood out as the last remaining critical public voice against the government. The military expelled two foreign priests working closely with the commission and threatened the bishops with possible expulsion of fourteen more foreign clerics if they did not reorganize the Justice and Peace Commission to stop its involvement in political affairs. Although a committee of the Episcopal

Conference had criticized the November decrees as "totalitarian" and contrary to the social principles of the Church regarding basic human rights,[49] as a group the bishops acquiesced to official demands. The government had closed down a Church-operated radio station in the mining region in January, and had also conducted further raids on bishops' houses in La Paz and Santa Cruz. In the context of this mounting attack on Church-affiliated organizations and personnel, and in light of the heavy dependence of the Church on foreign clergy, the bishops opted for a strategy of conciliation with the military and placed the Justice and Peace Commission in a state of recess.[50]

Thoughout 1975 mounting student and labor unrest and mining strikes occurred despite the government ban on political activities. The Conference of Religious Orders of Men and Women in Bolivia petitioned the bishops to assist the striking miners who had been fired, and in April in their monthly bulletin published an analysis of the loss of purchasing power and real income by miners, workers, and peasants due to currency devaluation, inflation, and controls on wages.[51] In late July three foreign nuns were expelled from the country for purportedly engaging in subversive political activity.

Finally, in December, 1976, the Episcopal Conference issued its first collective public criticism of the Banzer government. It criticized the very skewed distribution of wealth and unfair wage policies of the regime, which made the poor bear a disproportionate part of the cost of development. The bishops also attacked the model of the state being constructed by the military, which prolonged economic injustices by not allowing for adequate social participation by miners, peasants, and workers.[52]

In the same month, representatives of the Lutheran and Methodist churches and a priest from the Conference of Religious Orders of Men and Women met with several lay persons to form the Permanent Assembly of Human Rights in Bolivia. This ecumenical organization included in its stated goals the sensitizing of public opinion regarding human rights, the circulation of documents of reflection on statism and national security, and the defense of structures of participation (parties, unions, workers' and peasants' organizations).53 The Assembly received the blessing of both Cardinal Maurer of Sucre and Archbishop Manrique of La Paz, although it was not formally tied to Catholic and Protestant church structures. It immediately moved to establish financial ties with Protestant funding agencies in Europe and by August, 1977, had set up legal aid service for prisoners and their families as well as for miners fired from their jobs for striking and union activities. Similar to the former Justice and Peace Commission, it established regional offices in several other cities of the country, but with greater financial assistance and larger staff than its predecessor. In its publications it listed names of those killed in the last six years and has cited documented evidence of violations of such basic rights as the right to work, the right to education, the right to organize unions, the right to habeas corpus, and a fair trial.54 It also has urged general amnesty for all political prisoners and those in exile.

One major reason the Permanent Assembly has been able to continue its activities is that General Banzer in late 1977 announced that there would be general elections in July, 1978. Banzer has been conscious of U.S. interest and pressure to see democratic procedures reestablished in the country. This has made it harder for the government to repress dissent with the same amount of force as in

197

1975. In addition to the Permanent Assembly, many political, labor, and professional organizations have been active recently in pressuring the government to allow political exiles to return to the country for the election campaign. In late December six miners' wives, whose husbands are among this group (which numbers over fifteen thousand), began a hunger strike in the Chancery of the Archdiocese of La Paz. The strike soon spread to student, professional, and labor organizations in more than nine cities of the country, a total of more than a thousand people.[55]

The Permanent Assembly provided material support for the strikers and publicized their demands in newspaper ads.[56] Many of the participants gathered in churches in various dioceses. When troops invaded several of these buildings in La Paz and arrested clerical and lay participants of the movement, Archbishop Manrique threatened to place the archdiocese under a three-day interdict and excommunicate those conducting the attacks.[57] On January 18 General Banzer gave in to the demands of the hunger strike. He announced an amnesty for all political exiles and prisoners. He also said he would make no reprisals against hunger strikers or their supporters, would release the two hundred people already under arrest for having taken part in the movement, and would lift the ban on trade union activities. Public attention focused on preparing for the July elections and the hope for a civilian victory at the polls.[58]

Thus, Church activities for human rights in Bolivia since 1971 have been variegated and at times less than consistent. Only when the property or religious personnel of the institution have been under direct attack have the bishops been willing to confront the state openly, and then only on certain occasions. The traditional conservative orientation of the bishops, the lack of strong social commitment before the military coup, and the heavy dependence on foreign clergy have all made the hierarchy rather cautious in their defense of civil, social, and economic rights.

However, the clerics and religious at lower levels of the Catholic Church, especially in combination with lay Catholic and Protestant groups, have been able to mount some effective opposition to repression. Precisely because there is significant international pressure (particularly from the United States on the regime,[59] as well as some effective domestic secular opposition to the government, the strategies of the Permanent Assembly and other church leaders have been able to make some gains for civil and social rights.

The impact of those activities of the former Justice and Peace Commission and the current Permanent Assembly has perhaps been as problematic for the churches as for the government. Some Catholic bishops supported the efforts of the Permanent Assembly in the hunger strike, but these involved direct attacks on the churches themselves, and the government was in a much weaker position than before due to domestic and international pressures. The past record of the bishops, however, provides little evidence to believe the hierarchy will now become a consistent defender of civil, social, and economic rights of oppressed miners and peasants.

Furthermore, the actions of both the Justice and Peace Commission and the Permanent Assembly have precipitated some public divisions in the Catholic Church. In 1974, in 1977, and most recently during the 1978 hunger strike, a small group of diocesan clergy (predominantly Bolivians) issued public criticisms of religious order priests (overwhelmingly of foreign origin) for becoming involved in

politics and importing foreign ideology into the
country. In addition, after the hunger strike a
representative of the Latin American Anti-Communist Confederation (a right-wing Catholic
organization headquartered in Mexico) visited
Bolivia. In a press conference he accused Archbishop Manrique of being responsible for Communist
infiltration in the Bolivian Catholic Church. The
government media gave considerable attention to
these incidents, although the number of both
diocesan clergy and conservative laity ready to assist in this campaign against Church leaders and
foreign priests involved in human rights activities
in the country is relatively small.[60]

Finally, unlike the churches in Chile, Brazil,
and Paraguay, the Bolivian Church does not yet enjoy a significant network of small base communities
that can act as training grounds for indigenous lay
leaders. This means that the Church must still
depend heavily on foreign clergy to run its pastoral programs in the near future. This makes it
particularly vulnerable to government attack. It
also means that it cannot serve as an instrument
for social participation and consciousness-raising
at the local level with the same effectiveness as
do several other national churches in the subcontinent.

For all these reasons, although some significant
changes have occurred (especially in recent years),
chronic structural weaknesses and contradictions
persist in the Bolivian Church. These severely
limit its capacity to act as a consistent force
promoting human rights, except in certain crisis
situations.

V. Argentina: The Ecumenical Movement for Human Rights and the Permanent Assembly for Human Rights

Church responses to human rights violations in Argentina since the military coup in 1976 have been somewhat different from other countries in the southern region. Although Church leaders have spoken out against abuse of power and formed or participated in ecumenical organizations to promote human rights, their actions to date have been more circumscribed and their effectiveness more limited than that of their counterparts in neighboring countries. This is due mainly to the distinctive political situation and climate of insecurity that still prevail in the country.

In the late 1960's and early 1970's armed leftist movements emerged to oppose the military regime that took power in 1966--for example, the Montoneros and the People's Revolutionary Army (ERP). Through ransom from kidnappings, money stolen from banks, and assistance from abroad these organizations formed the best equipped and most effective guerrilla movement in Latin America by 1973. The withdrawal of the military from power in March, 1973, and the subsequent return of Juan Perón, proved a disillusionment for the Left. Two months after his death they resumed their armed struggle in September, 1974. During the year-and-a-half rule of Isabel Perón the country experienced severe economic difficulties, with inflation reaching an annual rate of 700 per cent by March, 1976. After 1974, however, a state of siege was also imposed, with more than 3,000 people placed in preventive detention. Private death squads, some of which were financed or assisted by the government itself, began to operate with impunity and were responsible for a large proportion of the 1,500 assassinations that occurred during the eighteen months following

201

Perón's death. The most infamous of these groups is the Argentine Anti-Communist Alliance (AAA), which has very close ties to the police and is responsible for over 300 murders in 1974 alone.[61]

Given this climate of terror, insecurity, and economic disruption, many Catholic bishops publicly welcomed and promised to support the government that took power in March, 1976.[62] The Church itself had suffered serious internal divisions during the late 1960's and early 1970's, when a group of several hundred priests actively opposed the former military regime and publicly urged major structural changes in the direction of a socialist economy. This movement had some positive impact on several bishops, but clashed with others.[63] By 1974 the organization had disbanded (itself suffering some of the attacks by the right-wing death squads), and the leadership of the Episcopal Conference was under control of conservatives who welcomed the return of the military.

In the months following the March coup, however, several events precipitated action by Church leaders on behalf of civil and political rights. The waves of killings and disappearances continued, and by November, 1976, the deaths totaled over 1,200.[64] These were perpetrated by both the Left and the Right. Many of those being persecuted and fired from their jobs flocked to churches for assistance and provided clear evidence to Church personnel of systematic use of torture by the military to extract information. By the end of the year at least twenty-five Catholic and Protestant clergy had been arrested and ten others assassinated by right-wing death squads.[65] Bishop Enrique Angelelli of La Rioja was killed mysteriously while collecting evidence concerning the deaths of two priests in his diocese who had been active in programs assisting the poor.[66]

Amidst this continuing violence and persecution of the churches themselves, the Catholic hierarchy issued a pastoral letter in May, 1976, condemning abuses of power. The bishops denied that the welfare of the state was above the rights of individuals and criticized the government for prolonged detentions, torture, denial of habeas corpus, and firing of workers for political reasons. They also stated that forcing others to go hungry "in order to gain unreasonable profit" was wrong, and that halting inflation too hurriedly at the expense of workers was a cardinal sin. The bishops, however, gave recognition to the delicate situation of the country and also condemned revolutionary uprising and "Marxist solutions to our problems."[67]

Two months later representatives of Catholic and Protestant churches formed the Ecumenical Movement for Human Rights (MEDH), an organization established to aid families of kidnapped persons and assist all those suffering the effects of "political and economic terrorism and indiscriminate repression." It included in its stated goals the preparation of documents concerning human rights violations, the formation of a body of lawyers to provide legal aid to those arrested and families of the disappeared, and communication with prisoners and other detainees.[68] It also has sought some financial assistance from international Catholic and Protestant organizations, but not to the extent of similar committees in Bolivia, Paraguay, and Chile. In Argentina any group with large amounts of outside funding is suspected of being a siphon for guerrilla support.

In addition to this ecumenical group another organization to defend human rights was established in late 1975 by some Protestant and Catholic leaders, along with intellectuals, professionals, and party representatives. This committee, known as the Permanent Assembly for Human Rights (APDH), documents cases of disappearances, presents legal petitions to the courts on behalf of those detained, and writes public letters to General Videla seeking investigations as to the whereabouts of those who are missing.[69] It has neither sought nor received substantial amounts of international funding for its activities.

To date the accomplishments of these two Church-related organizations have not been nearly as effective or publicized as the activities of ecumenical committees in Chile, Paraguay, and Bolivia. The Permanent Assembly has gathered well-documented evidence on cases of disappeared persons and the use of torture and has sought redress for victims of repression in the courts and from Videla himself.[70] The Ecumenical Movement has, in addition to offering legal aid, provided access to emergency relief for families of prisoners and the disappeared. There has been, however, very little response on the part of the courts and the government to legal petitions or requests by Church leaders for investigations.[71] There is good reason to believe that Videla himself does not wield effective control of the military and that strong right-wing elements in the armed forces and police act independently to perpetrate murder and torture. Conservative business groups seem to support these elements, and very repressive economic measures continue against workers and unions.

Furthermore, guerrilla activities also continue, and Videla uses this argument to justify further repression. In addition, over sixty lawyers have been assassinated since 1974, along with countless union and party leaders and those engaged in social programs assisting the poor. This in turn has forced Church-sponsored human rights organizations to act with extreme caution and keep a relatively low profile.

The impact of these new Church-sponsored organizations has sensitized Church leaders to the chronic problem of repression and has provided them with substantial documentation that kidnapping, murder, and torture originate more from government security forces than from guerrilla action. The hierarchy issued a second pastoral letter in May, 1977, partly as a result of this information, condemning these abuses by the government and criticizing violations of workers' rights to work, to health care, and to education. While reaffirming their rejection of Marxism, the bishops also stated that this does not justify branding as Marxists all who work for justice on behalf of the poor.[72]

Work for civil and political rights or for basic social assistance to the poor has precipitated continued attacks on Church personnel. By December, 1977, some thirty priests were in jail in Argentina, and at least seventeen have been murdered by security forces.[73] In this sense the Argentine situation resembles the Brazilian case of direct frontal attack on the churches themselves. The Argentine bishops, however, have been far more willing to communicate with the government and try to exercise influence behind the scenes than have their Brazilian counterparts. They still have hopes for Videla (a devout Catholic), they fear reprisals from right-wing security forces, and they are aware of the continued presence of guerrilla activities in the country. The Catholic Church in Argentina has not yet established a firm network of small base communities for evangelization and social participation that characterizes the Chilean, Brazilian, and Paraguayan churches.

For all these political and religious reasons,

the impact to date on human rights activities by Argentine churches has been the least effective of all other church groups in the subcontinent. The Catholic Church remains a weak and underdeveloped institution, with no past history of strong social commitment by the hierarchy. While it is slowly becoming sensitized to human rights issues as these directly affect its clergy and laity, the present prospects for the Church promoting civil, social, and economic rights are modest at best.

VI. Conclusions

Although there are characteristics peculiar to each of these new Church pastoral and social organizations in the five countries, some common patterns can be identified. These pertain to the three issues raised in the introduction to this paper: (1) how and why churches have become involved in human rights activities in the subcontinent; (2) the scope and extent of their work; and (3) the impact of these new structures on both society and the churches themselves.

All five cases indicate that Church programs for human rights are basically reactive strategies, responding to unforeseen crises in secular society. The policy of promoting human rights (although legitimized in the Medellín documents of 1968) did not become a conscious priority of any of the national hierarchies until they were stimulated to act by pressures from below in their own churches or from outside the ecclesiastical institutions. In some cases the killing of clergy moved the bishops to set up emergency programs; in others, direct attacks on already existing Church programs benefiting the poor moved them. In many situations, however, the response came from general public pressure, as many people had nowhere else to go for help and the churches were the last remaining or-

ganizations with any relative degree of freedom to
act.

In all these countries the international link-
ages of the churches gave them an important
capacity for action. Access to finances and
material support in both Western Europe and the
United States enabled them to begin humanitarian
projects to assist the persecuted. In turn, the
information on rights violations to which religious
personnel had access by direct experience could be
effectively and swiftly communicated through the
international network of the churches themselves.
Without such ability to transfer money, material,
and information across national borders these new
Church-sponsored programs could not have been begun or sustained.

Some of these churches clearly are learning from
one another and making efforts to share experiences
and strategies within the southern tier region itself. This process is facilitated by the growing
network of communication and exchange of religious
and lay personnel across national borders, which
makes churches one of the few effective private
transnational actors in the region capable of
counteracting the international reach of the military. The growing ecumenical cooperation between
Catholics and Protestants in Latin America also en-
hances the structural capacities of all Christian
denominations to combine efforts and promote rights
activities. In fact, much of the financing for
these new human rights committees in Catholic countries comes from Protestant sources in Western
Europe and North America.

Regarding the scope and extent of activities of
these new programs, it is clear that most of the
aid they provide goes for the defense of classic
civil rights--the right of habeas corpus, the right

to a fair trial, the right to be protected against torture. A broad consensus exists on the legitimacy of these individual rights--especially among funding agencies in Europe and the United States. The programs are also able to perform humanitarian functions, such as allowing prison visits, improving the living situation in jails, enhancing communication between those detained and their families, and providing, food, clothing, and health care for families. In some instances (such as the Chilean, Brazilian, and Paraguayan cases), churches have been able to promote some social and economic rights--for example, the right to work or the right to participate in social organizations of one's own choice.

In no case, however, have the churches been able by themselves to affect major changes in the political and economic structures underlying or causing the violations of civil, social, and economic rights. Where changes have occurred in patterns of repression (e.g., in Paraguay), they have been due primarily to pressures by foreign governments, or in conjunction with foreign pressure and activity by both religious and secular domestic forces within the countries themselves (e.g., in Bolivia). Even in such cases it is too soon to predict whether a fundamental reorientation of political and economic institutions will occur or whether this "decompression" is merely a transitory concession. Furthermore, where military regimes are strongly entrenched and unyielding to foreign and domestic opposition to their policies (e.g., in Chile and Brazil), not even momentary amelioration has been achieved by the churches.

What these human rights committees and other new pastoral programs of the churches among the poor have accomplished over the past several years, however, is the sensitizing of many bishops, clergy, and religious to the close relationship between the existing unequal arrangement of economic and political power and the systematic violation of civil rights of individuals and groups. In almost all of the major episcopal documents on human rights originating from the subcontinent recently there has been a strong appeal for changes in basic institutional structures and more equitable distribution of wealth and resources in order to remove the causes of murder, torture, and kidnapping.

The bishops see very clearly that those being persecuted are predominantly spokespersons for the poor or working-class leaders themselves. A major reason for their being attacked, claim the bishops, is their demand that society meet the basic human needs of its people in a more just fashion--employment, housing, education, and health care. Now that guerrilla activity has subsided significantly throughout the region, the primary reason for repression is that the poor are demanding social and economic rights. The hierarchies, therefore, emphasize the necessity of affecting changes in economic development models based on national security ideology and manipulated by élites toward other strategies of development, which include more equitable distribution of land and income as they proceed. They also stress the importance of allowing intermediary structures of social and political participation (e.g., labor unions, political parties, civic and professional associations or neighborhood groups) between the state and the individual, both to affect such changes and to provide accountability of power.

Despite these arguments on the close interrelationship of defense of civil rights, fulfillment of human needs, and responsible uses of power, there is no indication that the bishops' words are, or will be, taken seriously in the near future by those

controlling economic resources or wielding coercive
authority. But such pronouncements nevertheless
are important because they provide an alternative
moral perspective and force that challenge the
legitimacy and pervasiveness of national security
ideology underlying all of these rights violations.
An important power of the Church, therefore, lies
at the deeper ideological and spiritual level. The
influence is potentially very great, since Christianity is deeply embedded in Latin American culture, and people, even if they do not practice
their religion regularly, still have emotional ties
to the Church. This is particularly true for
middle-class groups and the poor themselves. Not
only have the hierarchies refused to give complete
legitimation to national security regimes (as they
often did to earlier authoritarian or oligarchic
governments in Latin America), but the latent moral
force of the Church (which is most notable in
crisis situations) is helping to prevent the values
and symbols of this new secular ideology from gaining complete public acceptance.

In addition to this moral contribution to the
defense of human rights in the subcontinent, the
other most significant accomplishment of the Church
at the domestic level has been to provide alternate
forms of participation that can nourish a critical
consciousness as well as a spirit of resistance
among Indians, peasants, and workers. The new
small communities and other lay training programs
in the churches are acting as social incubators for
future generations of leaders of the poor, and are
providing them with a sense of hope and solidarity.
These organizations are counterproductive to the
efforts by dictatorial regimes attempting to construct a new model of society and new type of person completely dominated by state power and terror.
In the long run these are probably the most significant contributions Latin American churches are

making to effect eventual structural transformations and return to democratic procedures. At the
very least they are blunting the impact of repression generated by both the military and economic
élites to maintain their power.

In an immediate sense, the impact of these new
programs on the churches themselves has been profound. In some instances the programs have
precipitated outright persecution that reaches the
highest level of Church leadership. This has
helped to sensitize many bishops to the plight of
the lower clergy, religious, and working-class
laity in a way that would not have been possible
otherwise. Further, these experiences are making
them aware, for the first time, that the real
threat to the institutional interests of the
Church comes from the Right and not the Left. It
is shifting the priorities of the Church to a
closer identification with the poor, since these
people make the most pressing demands on the
Church's time and resources, while showing the
greatest willingness to participate in its new
evangelical efforts.

Serious internal tensions and contradictions
have resulted from these new directions in the
Church, which place important limits on how far efforts to defend human rights can go. Upper-middle-
class groups, reactionary Catholics, and military
officers are by and large outraged at this betrayal
by Church leaders of their interests. These groups
wield considerable influence not only in secular
society but within the Church itself, since they
still provide significant financial support for
other Church-sponsored activities--schools, hospitals, charity funds, and the like. They can also
mount effective terror campaigns against Church
personnel (as witness TFP activities in Chile,
Brazil, and Argentina), while exploiting internal

211

divisions in the hierarchy and clergy.

A primary Catholic concern (reinforced stongly
by the Vatican) is to maintain the public unity of
the institution at all possible costs, while remaining open to minister to the spiritual needs of
all classes of people. The Catholic Church has
traditionally opted for a church rather than sect
model of religious development, and this places
theological limitations on its prophetic capacities
as well as on its ability to represent the interests
of any one social group forcefully and consistently.
Both political and religious factors, therefore,
influence the official policies of churches as
articulated by bishops. They do not want to alien-
ate élite groups any more than necessary and are
not likely to write them off on behalf of human
rights programs that bring an all-out conflict between the Church and secular power.

Furthermore, as was seen in the case of Bolivia
in relation to the clergy, and in Chile and
Argentina in regard to money, international sources
of support for human rights programs create some
problems for the Church at the domestic level. Not
only are some indigenous groups within the local
churches suspicious of those with access to
resources (and, therefore, power) from abroad, but
the military governments of these countries are
sensitive to foreign influences due to their
exaggerated sense of nationalism. While this dependency of the churches has not yet become a major
limitation on Church programs, it certainly has
caused tension. It is also probable that this vul-
nerability in terms of foreign personnel and
finances will be another factor keeping bishops from
allowing an all-out confrontation between Church
and state on behalf of human rights.

Finally, despite recent commitments to the inter-

ests of the poor and new working-class receptiveness
to Church activities and participation, all of the
churches in the southern region have only begun the
process of penetrating and understanding lower-class
culture. Small base communities are just beginning
to take root, and the vast majority of poor still
have little formal contact with the churches.
Churches are, on the whole, very underdeveloped institutions in this area. It will be some time before new communities can function effectively and
autonomously sufficient to withstand sustained
frontal attacks on their personnel by repressive
governments.

The important factor, however, is that these new
programs have started to operate. Moreover, given
the clear intentions of the military to stay in
power for a long time, the programs analyzed here
are more than short-term emergency efforts. If both
international pressure and cautious diplomacy by the
bishops can prevent prolonged Church-state confronta-
tions, they may very well grow stronger. Such new
grassroots structures could be important instruments
for bringing about long-term change in both Church
and society. The Church, therefore, while not a
consistent or strong defender of rights, provider
of needs, or instrument of power, does wield some
crucial moral and structural influence in this
region of the continent--influence that may be quite
significant for the future direction of these societies.

Notes

1. José Comblín, "La doctrine de la seguridad nacional," and Albert Methol Ferré, "Sobre la actual ideología de la seguridad nacional," in *Dos Ensayos Sobre Seguridad Nacional*, 2 vols. (Santiago: Vicaría de la Solidaridad, 1977).

The protection of national security has been emphasized by these military regimes in their attempts to provide themselves with a sense of legitimacy and justification for systematic repression. National security ideology includes among its major components anti-Marxism, patriotism, technocratic value-free planning, and the subordination of personal rights to the interests of the state.

2. *The Amnesty International Report, 1975-76* (London: Amnesty International Publications, 1976); "Report of an Amnesty International Mission to Argentina," Amnesty International Publications, 15 November 1976, pp. 7-10.

Several international organizations have documented these violations on the basis of on-site fact-finding investigations and personal testimonies of individuals or groups within these Latin American countries. Included are Amnesty International, the International League of Human Rights, the International Commission of Jurists, the Commission on Human Rights of the United Nations Economic and Social Council, and the Inter-American Commission on Human Rights. Amnesty International, for example, in its 1975-76 annual report, indicated that 80 per cent of all reported incidents of serious torture to date have occurred in Latin America.

3. Robert A. Mitchell, "Latin American Bishops Speak: Human Rights, Needs and Power" (unpublished essay. Washington, D.C.: Woodstock Theological Center, 1977).

Two very useful collections of fourteen of these documents have recently been published in English by the Latin American Documentation Service of the U.S. Catholic Conference. See references for individual citations in the LADOC "Keyhole" Series.

Mitchell provides an excellent summary of the general analysis and principles laid out in these documents regarding the interrelationship of human rights, human needs, and political and economic power.

4. Argentine Episcopal Conference, "The Common Good and the Present Situation," USCC, LADOC Keyhole Series 15, 1977, pp. 16-21; Chilean Episcopal Conference, "Our Life as a Nation," USCC LADOC Keyhole Series 15, 1977, pp. 41-54; National Conference of Brazilian Bishops, "Pastoral Message to the People of God," USCC, LADOC Keyhole Series 15, 1977, pp. 21-35.

5. CELAM (Council of Latin American Bishops), "Peace," in *The Church in the Present Day Transformation of Latin America in the Light of the Council*, vol. 2 (Bogotá: General Secretariat of CELAM, 1970), pp. 80-81.

This new emphasis in the Church toward service to the world, especially the poor, was officially endorsed in the documents of the Second Vatican Council (1962-65), as well as by the Latin American bishops themselves in their second General Conference held in Medellín, Colombia, in August, 1968. At this meeting representatives of every episcopal conference in Latin America committed the Church to act as a "catalyst in the temporal realm in an authentic attitude of service." As pastors they dedicated themselves "to denounce everything which, opposing justice destroys peace," "to defend the rights of the poor and oppressed," and "to encourage and favor efforts of the people to create and develop their own grass-roots organizations for the consolidation of their rights and the search for justice."

6. Although Paraguay has not recently come under military rule, the twenty-four-year-old military government of General Stroessner in the last two years has escalated its repressive measures considerably against *campesino* leaders. The Paraguayan churches responded to this recent increase in terror by setting up an Emergency Committee on Human Rights.

Despite systematic violation of human rights by the Uruguayan Government since the 1973 civil-military coup, religious groups have not been able to establish programs to promote human rights comparable to those in sister churches in other areas of the Southern Cone. The reasons for this are the long-standing weakness of the Uruguayan Church, the heavily secularized culture in Uruguay, and the effective neutralization of the Church by an alliance among conservative Catholics, the press, and the military.

In Peru the military have not been guilty of violations of human rights (especially civil rights) to the same degree as their counterparts in Brazil, Chile, Argentina, Paraguay, Bolivia, and Uruguay. In the last two years, however, very repressive social and economic measures (particularly against workers in the form of wage controls and restrictions of union activities) have occurred. While the Church has not felt it necessary to establish human rights committees specifically to meet the needs of prisoners or families of disappeared persons, the bishops have begun to criticize severely the economic policies of the government along the same lines as the hierarchies in Brazil, Chile, and Argentina. (See Penny Lernoux, "Church Cowed by Uruguayan Military," Report to Alicia Patterson Foundation, 18 January 1977 {memo}; Eugene K. Culhane, "Strange Alliance in Uruguay," *America*, 17 May 1975, pp. 282-83; "Government Bars Bishops' Letter on Violence in Uruguay," *Latinamerica Press*, 16 October 1975, p. 1; "Bishops Challenge Peru's

Economic Policies," *Latinamerica Press*, 21 July 1977, pp. 3, 4, 8.)

7. "Declaración de comité permanente del episcopado sobre la situación del país," in *Documentos de Episcopado, Chile, 1970-1973*, ed. C. Oviedo Cavada (Santiago: Ediciones Mundo, 1974), p. 174.

8. Two bishops were responsible for inaugurating this commission--Auxiliary Bishop Fernando Ariztía of the Western Zone of the Catholic Archdiocese of Santiago and Bishop Helmut Frenz of the Lutheran Church of Chile. Both men had been particularly active in programs helping poor before the coup and had been exposed to many cases of cruelty against their people in the days immediately following September 11. Frenz was also a German and had direct access to immediate funding from Western Europe, including the World Council of Churches in Geneva. Both of these men urged other Catholic, Protestant, and Jewish leaders to join them (including Cardinal Silva), and together they formally established the Committee of Cooperation for Peace on October 6, 1973. Ariztía and Frenz served as co-chairpersons.

9. Between October, 1973, and December, 1975, the various projects sponsored or assisted by funds coming through the Committee for Peace reached over 100,000 people needing legal, medical, or economic assistance, in addition to those workers assisted by 126 small enterprises set up in various parts of the country. (U.S. Congress, House, Subcommittee on International Organizations of the Committee on International Relations, "Prepared statement of José Zalaquett Daher, chief legal counsel, Committee of Cooperation for Peace in Chile," *Chile: The Status of Human Rights and Its Relationship to U.S. Economic Assistance Programs*, 94th Cong., 2d sess., 1976, p. 59.)

10. Vicaría de la Solidaridad, "Vicaría de la

solidaridad: un año de labor," Santiago, January, 1977, mimeo.

11. Katherine Gilfeather, "Women in Ministry," *America*, 2 October 1976, pp. 191-94.
Many of the self-help projects in these local communities (e.g., soup kitchens) are also assisted by the Vicariate of Solidarity.

12. Sociedad Chilena de Defensa de la Tradición, Familia y Propiedad, *La Iglesia del Silencio en Chile* (Santiago: Edunsa, 1976).

13. "La Inter-American Foundation y sus programas en Chile," *El Mercurio* (Santiago), 25 January 1978, p. 24.

14. Comité Permanente del Episcopado de Chile, "Evangelo y Paz," *Mensaje*, 24 (October, 1975): 462-73.

15. Chilean Episcopal Conference, "Our Life as a Nation," USCC, LADOC Keyhole Series 15, 1977, pp. 41-54.

16. Not only did high inflation, corruption, and incompetence characterize the democratic regime of João Goulart between 1961 and 1964, but many in the country felt that Communists had a strong possibility of taking over the country as a result of this turmoil. With the exception of Chile and Cuba, the Brazilian Left was the best organized Marxist movement in Latin America in the early 1960's, especially in rural areas of the northeast. (Thomas C. Bruneau, *The Political Transformation of the Brazilian Catholic Church* {London: Cambridge University Press, 1974}, pp. 66, 93, 181.)

17. Bruneau, p. 124.

18. Ibid., p. 126.

19. Between 1966 and 1971 several conflicts between government and some bishops and priests oc-

curred when the latter began to criticize publicly the economic policies of the government, which favored industrial development at the expense of social programs to assist the poor in interior regions. By 1969 eleven foreign priests had been expelled (of over five thousand in the country) and one priest closely associated with Dom Helder Camara had been assassinated.

20. CNBB (Conferencia Nacional dos Bispos do Brasil), "Documento pastoral do Brasilia," *Revista Eclesiastica Brasiliera*, 30 (June, 1970): 415. An English translation of the section dealing with repression and torture appears in *LADOC*, 1, no. 13 (June, 1970).

21. "Operation Hope," begun by Dom Helder Camara, is one of the best-known examples of grass-roots self-help programs in northeastern Brazil. Begun in 1967, it has sponsored projects in literacy training, housing, health, and recreation in thirteen urban and rural communities in the Recife-Olinda diocese. Materials and salaries for specialists are provided by the West German bishops, but most of the participants are volunteers. In addition to basic humanitarian aid, there has been a consistent emphasis on raising the social consciousness of the people. Small group discussions of community problems, identification of desirable social and economic objectives, and petitions to local authorities for better services have all become integral parts of this program. (Marjorie Hope, "The People's Priest," *Lithopinion* {New York}, Spring, 1975, p. 46.)

22. Agostino Bono, "Cross vs. Sword: Catholic Aid to Poor in Brazil Is Worsening Conflict With Military," *Wall Street Journal*, 2 June 1977, p. 1.

23. Estudos de CNBB, *Pastoral Social*, no. 10 (São Paulo: Ediçaoes Paulinas, 1976).

24. Hope, p. 54; Bono, p. 20.

25. Tad Szulc, "'Recompression' in Brazil," *New Republic*, 7 May 1977, p. 19.

26. Thousands of Indians and peasants have been living on these lands for years and therefore qualify for ownership by law. Nevertheless, they have never obtained legal titles from the government and now are being evicted, and in some cases murdered, by both security forces and private land developers. (Estudos de CNBB, *Pastoral de Terra*, no. 11 {São Paulo: Ediçaoes Paulinas, 1976}.)

27. This situation of "decompression," begun after President Ernesto Geisel took office in 1974, was only in part due to urging by the Church. The accumulated effects of rapid economic growth (primarily favoring the upper and middle-income sectors) and organized terrorism since 1968 have solidified the power of the government. The present administration could easily afford to ease up on some of the repression and make concessions, as none of these changes would create a serious threat to military power, and tight control is still maintained over the major decisionmaking centers of society.

28. National Conference of Brazilian Bishops, "Christian Requirements of a Political Order," USCC, LADOC Keyhole Series 16, 1977, pp. 54-67; National Conference of Brazilian Bishops, "Pastoral Message to the People of God," LADOC Keyhole Series 15, 1976, pp. 21-35.

29. Roberto Barbosa, "Issue of Communism in Church-State Relations in Brazil," *LADOC*, 8, no. 3 (January-February, 1978): 27.
Security dossiers are now prepared on bishops and priests identified with these new Church-sponsored communities and programs. Among the questions included in the two-page questionnaire to be

completed by police agents are: Does the bishop or priest try to disfigure the person of Christ? Does he try to disfigure the person of God? Does he talk about *comunidades de base?*

30. "Sigaud Versus Casaldaliga and Balduino," *LADOC*, 8, no. 3 (January-February, 1978), p. 15.

31. Jorge Domínguez, "Smuggling," *Foreign Policy*, Fall, 1975, pp. 95-96.

32. Ben S. Stephansky and Robert J. Alexander, "Report of the Commission of Enquiry Into Human Rights in Paraguay of the International League for Human Rights, July 6-15, 1976," U.S. Congress, House, Subcommittee on International Organizations of the Committee on International Relations, *Human Rights in Uruguay and Paraguay*, 94th Cong., 2d sess., 1976, p. 161.

33. Stephansky and Alexander, p. 174.

34. Ibid., p. 180.

35. A priest with first-hand knowledge of deacon programs told me of his admiration for the men training to be deacons who return to groups time and again even after being arrested and tortured.

36. Episcopal Conference of Paraguay, "Amidst Persecutions and Consolations," USCC, LADOC Keyhole Series 15, 1977, pp. 7, 9, 10, 11.

37. Ibid., p. 14; Stephansky and Alexander, p. 209.
One of the key government strategies used to discredit the churches is to accuse priests and ministers of betraying their ministry and acting as guerrilla agents. The chief of the security police, Pastor Coronel, made a report to the Colorado party in 1976 naming several missionaries as conspirators in a clandestine movement known as the OPM (Organización Politico Militar). In addition, the government has produced a number of popular pamphlets and catechisms to be used in religious classes in pub-

lic schools in which communism is presented as the cardinal sin for Christians, and images and activities of "bad priests" are sketched and rejected as being against true religion. (Ministerio de Educación y Culto, "Estudiando felices sin comunismo," and "Las verdades anticomunistas de hoy" {Asunción, Paraguay: Ministerio de Educación y Culto, 1977}, mimeo.)

38. "Paraguay Churches Unite Their Efforts," *LADOC*, 6, no. 65 (July-August, 1976), p. 19.

39. Ben S. Stephansky and David M. Helfield, "Denial of Human Rights in Paraguay: Report of the Second Commission of Enquiry of the International League for Human Rights (New York: International League for Human Rights, December, 1977), p. 4.

40. Margaret D. Wilde, "Paraguayans Savor Christian Solidarity," *The Christian Century*, 94 (30 March 1977): 301; Comité de las Iglesias, *Boletín Informativo*, no. 1 (May,1977), p. 6; no. 2 (July, 1977), p. 6.

In February, 1977, Cardinal Evaristo Arns of São Paulo, Brazil, personally visited the office of the Committee of Churches for Emergency Aid in a spirit of fraternal solidarity, only the third Roman Catholic cardinal ever to visit the country. He held a press conference with Archbishop Rolon of Asunción, and both praised the committee publicly for its important work. Other Protestant and Catholic church people from Western Europe and North America have also visited the committee over the past two years, and thus have added to its reputation, in the eyes of the Paraguayan Government, as being internationally supported.

41. Comité de las Iglesias, *Boletín Informativo*, no. 3 (September, 1977), pp. 3-4.

42. David Vidal, "Paraguay Enjoys Old Siestas and the New Boom," *New York Times*, 18 February 1978, p. 6.

43. Roberto Barbosa, "New Hope for Paraguay's Prisoners," *Christian Century*, 94 (30 March 1977): 302.

Stephansky and Helfield in their latest report for the International League of Human Rights concluded that:

Notwithstanding the indications of amelioration, we found no compelling evidence of change either in the overall gravity of the human rights crisis or in the character of the basic institutions underlying that crisis.

Most importantly, the institutions that are at the root of the repressions of last year remain unchanged.

What our mission encountered was an interlude of amelioration, a welcome one to be sure, but nevertheless an interlude to an uncertain future. There have been interludes before, of the kind we encountered, for example, in the periods that preceded episodes of repression of 1958-1959, of 1965 and of 1969, as well as the period that preceded the most recent repressions of 1975-1976. Whether the present interlude will end with another repressive episode in a continuing cycle of repression and alleviation, or whether it can mark the beginning of an era of more durable government, will depend on governmental decisions yet to be taken {Stephansky and Helfield, pp. 12, 17, 18}.

44. CEP (Centro de Estudios y Publicaciones), *Bolivia: 1971-1976; Pueblo, Estado, Iglesia* (Lima: CEP, 1976), p. 22.

45. Bolivia has one of the highest percentages of foreign-born priests of all Latin American churches, with 80 per cent of the clergy coming from abroad.

46. CEP, p. 53.

47. Ibid., p. 67.

I am most grateful to the Reverend Eric de Wasseige, O.P., for much of this information on the Justice and Peace Commission of Bolivia. He worked on this commission for two years before being expelled from Bolivia in March, 1975.

48. Ibid., p. 150.

49. Ibid., p. 132.

50. Ibid., p. 161. The Commission was later reopened but placed under the direct control of the hierarchy and was constituted by a more conservative group of laity and clerics than its predecessor.

51. Ibid,, pp. 95, 186.

52. Centro de Proyección Cristiana, "Documento del episcopado Boliviano sobre la misión de la Iglesia ante la sociedad histórica del país," in *Los Derechos Humanos hoy en Latinoamérica: las declaraciones y documentos de la Iglesia universal y las Naciones Unidas* (Lima: Centro de Proyección Cristiana, 1977), p. 22.

53. "Primera reunión de la Asamblea Permanente de los Derechos Humanos en Bolivia" (La Paz, 22 December 1976, mimeo); "Bolivians Seek Democracy and Freedom," *LADOC*, 8, no. 3 (January-February, 1978), pp. 44-47.

54. Asamblea Permanente de los Derechos Humanos de Bolivia, "La declaración universal de los derechos humanos y la represión en Bolivia" (La Paz, October, 1977, mimeo).

55. "Bolivia: Heavens Above," *Latin America Political Report*, 13 January 1978, p. 12; *Lucha* (South Bend, Ind.), "Bolivian Hunger Strike," January-February, 1978, p. 21.

56. As the hunger strike spread, so did the demands of the participating groups. These included a withdrawal of military personnel from mining

villages, restoration of union rights, and the re-
hiring of miners fired for strike activities.
(Asamblea Permanente de los Derechos Humanos de
Bolivia, "20 días de huelga de hambre!" *Presencia*
{La Paz}, 15 January 1978.)

57. "Bolivia: The Will of the People," *Latin America Political Report*, 27 January 1978, p. 29.

58. Several civilian candidates competed in the
July, 1978, elections against the hand-picked candidate of Banzer, General Pareda Asbún. The latter
won the election, but, according to reports by international observer teams, only with the help of
massive fraud. Amidst mounting domestic and international pressures for a new election, a week later
General Pareda Asbún engineered a countercoup (very
possibly at Banzer's suggestion). Hence, once more,
democratic procedures were thwarted, despite strong
efforts by both domestic and international groups
to the contrary.

59. "Bolivia: Delaying Tactics," *Latin America
Political Report*, 10 February 1978, p. 46.
Some observers in Bolivia believe that the really effective check on Banzer in early 1978 was a
public remark made by the U.S. AID director in
Bolivia at that time: "President Carter believes
that the Bolivian electoral process in 1978 is very
important, not only for Bolivia, but for the whole
of Latin America."

60. "Clero diocesano pronuncia sobre la misión de
la Iglesia," *El Diario* (La Paz), 29 January 1978;
"Relaciones sobre la infiltración comunista en la
Iglesia Boliviana," *El Diario*, 7 February 1978.

61. Amnesty International, "Report of an Amnesty
International Mission to Argentina" (Amnesty International Publications, 15 November 1976), p. 7.

62. CELADEC (Comisión Evangélica Latinoamérica de
Educación Cristiana), *Iglesia Argentina: Fidelidad*

al evangelio? (Lima: CELADEC, 1977), p. 40.

63. Michael Dodson, "Religious Innovation and the Politics of Argentina: A Study of the Movement of Priests for the Third World" (Ph.d. dissertation, Indiana University, 1973).
The best account of the origins and development of this organization, known as "Movement of Priests for the Third World," has been written by Dodson.

64. CELADEC, p. 34.

65. "Church Members Under Attack," *Argentina Outreach*, January-February, 1977, p. 16.

66. Catholic Institute for International Relations, *Death and Violence in Argentina* (London: Catholic Institute for International Relations, 1976), p. 5.
The deaths occurred in an area of the country where the right-wing Catholic organization "Tradition, Family and Fatherland" is active and after Bishop Angelelli had spoken against the military coup.

67. "The Common Good and the Present Situation," USCC, LADOC Keyhole Series 15, 1976, pp. 18-19.

68. Movimiento Ecuménico por los Derechos Humanos, "Documento Base" (Buenos Aires, 9 June 1976, mimeo).

69. Andrew Brewin, Louis Duclos, and David McDonald, "One Gigantic Prison" (Toronto: Inter-Church Committee on Chile, November, 1976, mimeo).
Bishop Carlos Gattinoni of the Methodist Church was chosen as the first president of the Permanent Assembly, and Monsignors Jaime de Nevares and Enrique Angelelli (died 1976) also became members of the coordinating committee when the Assembly was formed.

70. "APDH Seeks Disappearance Probe," *Buenos Aires Herald*, 12 August 1977; "Human Rights Assembly Petitions the President," *Buenos Aires Herald*, 23 March 1977; "Armed Band Seizes Members of Argentina

Multichurch Group," *Latinamerica Press*, 22 December 1977, pp. 1-2.

71. In January, 1978, the government did acknowledge that it was holding 3,700 people and began to release some of their names. This concession, however, seems to have been the result of international pressure by the governments of France and the United States more than domestic church appeals. The French Government increased diplomatic pressure on Argentina after two French nuns were kidnapped in December, 1977. U.S. Secretary of State Vance made a trip to Argentina in late 1977 and also expressed this country's extreme concern over the human rights situation in Argentina. President Carter, during his visit to France in December, 1977, stated publicly: "The Argentine situation is the most serious of our continent." ("Argentina: Whose Balloon?" *Latin America Political Report*, 3 February 1978, p. 38.)

72. Argentina Episcopal Conference, "A Christian Reflection for the People of Argentina," USCC, LADOC Keyhole Series 16, 1977, pp. 26, 27, 29.

73. "Argentina: War of Words," *Latin America Political Report*, 3 December 1977, pp. 397-99.

THE CULTURAL FACTOR REAPPRAISED

WILLIAM L. BRADLEY

We conclude this study with many of our misgivings
unresolved. Our hearts tell us that we must attempt
somehow to make manifest our belief in universal human rights by extending to others the benefits that
have been granted us by accident of birth. Yet
there is nothing in this volume that demonstrates
concretely how the United States can implement its
idealism toward the citizens of other nations where
there is resistance by the sovereign authority. In
our progression from theological to legal to historical and cultural considerations of the issue,
we have been shown, first, that within the natural
law tradition of Western Christendom, individual
rights have been held secondary to the enhancement
of the common good; second, that there has never
been a time in human history when a single set of
cultural norms could specify what is good for every
person; and third, that American ambivalence regarding the imposition of our moral standards on other
states is as old as the nation itself.

Our discussions of particular societies have
served to emphasize the problems that our government must face in trying to apply its moral idealism in particular situations. Does it clarify or
confuse the issue to be shown the cultural continuity between the old Russia and the new, where
physical survival required a rigid social structure

in which the interests of individuals are subordinated to those of society? Does it help us to know that the traditional ethos of the Great Russians is more consistently represented by the present Soviet leadership than by the Westernized dissidents of czarist and Communist Russia? Are we relieved to learn that we can mute our democratic message to the People's Republic of China because individual liberties have never been considered paramount throughout the more than two millennia of Chinese civilization? How do we approach the new nations of Africa, whose precolonial societies in many ways gave more freedom and respect to the individual than does our own, but whose present governments are often repressive and authoritarian, and whose national boundaries, artificially created by Western imperialism, conflict with ancient tribal configurations? What should be our posture toward Islamic nations like Iran, breaking the chains of oppression in favor of a theocratic state that may limit the freedom of certain classes whom the shah had seemed to liberate from ancient restrictions imposed upon them by religious law? Where do we stand on the freedom movements in Latin America; with the religious conservatism that is grounded in long-standing traditional sources or with the liberation theology that draws sustenance from secular Marxism?

While we gave serious attention to the cultures and historical traditions of nations strongly affected by the American interest in universal human rights, we might well have looked more closely at the diversity of Christian theological positions that help to shape our judgments about the place of human rights in international diplomacy. The pluralistic character of Christian theology allows for diverse and often contradictory interpretations of the right relationship between society and the individual. Orthodox theology makes for a sharp

230

distinction between the religious and secular roles of church and state and grants the governing authority, be it monarchist, Communist, militarist, or democratic, *carte blanche* over the secular affairs of its citizens; accordingly, it has little to say about individual human rights under the state. Classical Roman Catholic theology, whose social doctrines stem from Aristotle's definition of man as a social animal and St. Thomas's hierarchical ordering of society, defines the individual by his place within the social order; his freedom, therefore, derives from his vocation rather than his individuality. Calvinism, being theocratic like Islam, maintains that freedom is a conferred rather than a natural right that may, in fact, have been predestined by an inscrutable Lawgiver. Liberal Protestantism, rooted in the philosophies of Locke and Kant and the theology of Schleiermacher, sees all rights vested in the individual, as does the secular political liberalism derived from the Enlightenment. Neo-orthodox theology, a product of the political and cultural turmoil of the period between the two world wars, trusts neither in the perfectibility of society nor the innocence of the individual, but sees a shifting balance between the two in a constant dialectical tension expressed politically by the manipulation of power. Existential theology, arising from European despair at midcentury, stresses individual freedom and responsibility against an impersonal, mechanical society in a universe devoid of charts or guideposts. The newest of the schools, liberation theology, has grown out of the efforts of religious leaders to identify themselves with freedom movements in Latin America, the United States, and Southern Africa; it is rooted biblically in the Exodus theme of the Old Testament. This theological movement is the protagonist of human rights for the impoverished and oppressed in every society, opposing the rights of the poor against the entrenched interests of the

231

affluent. Like classical Marxism it places the interests of disinherited classes above those of
sovereign states.

With so many variants of theology on which to
ground one's social philosophy, the Christian can
find justification for almost any conceivable position on human rights, whether it be the validation
of apartheid by a Calvinist Afrikaner, the use of
terror by a mission-educated freedom fighter, the
silent compliance with political suppression by a
Russian patriarch, or clandestine opposition to the
state by a Russian Baptist. Sincere Christians support the despotism of military governments as a
lesser evil, while others just as sincerely support
revolutions directed against them. In this there
are many precedents in history, not the least of
which was Luther's opposition to the peasants' rebellion; his belief in liberty did not extend to
the support of political disorder.

In this century American religious thought has
been dominated successively by three schools of
theology: liberalism, neo-orthodoxy, and liberation
theology. Despite their significant differences,
each takes its starting point from the Pilgrim theme
that America is a chosen people, called out of a
wicked land to create a new society that shall be a
model to all peoples of the earth. Liberalism identified the myth with American democracy, neo-orthodoxy repudiated it as a mark of unwarranted national pride, and liberation theology has reinterpreted
it to signify the oppressed classes within American
society. During the period of liberalism we believed in our national innocence and in our divine
mandate to extend the democratic way of life by
peaceful means throughout the world. In our period
of disillusionment, occasioned by the failure of
the League of Nations to maintain peace, the failure of the economic system to maintain prosperity,

232

and the rise of dictatorial militarism in Germany,
Italy, and Japan, neo-orthodoxy taught us that
power is the critical component in all political relationships and that our type of democratic freedom
can be preserved and extended only by the clear-
headed management of power. Disillusionment with
the realistic politics that failed to preserve us
from the mistakes of military involvement in Indochina gave rise to the theology of liberation, a
school that has returned to the Exodus theme of the
chosen people of God--the theme of the Pilgrim
colonists--but has limited the chosen to the "Third
and Fourth World" peoples, the neglected and often
exploited and oppressed classes, who exist in every
country.

Liberation theology strikes a response in us because as Americans we are heirs to the vision of a
world of peace and freedom in which men and women
have the liberty and encouragement to pursue their
individual interests without unwarranted interference from the state. We are attracted by the theme
in part because of a burden of guilt borne by Americans as by no other people for the poverty and in-
equity that exist throughout the world. As bene-
ficiaries of the technological revolution that has
transformed the earth in the last two centuries, we
are mindful that most of mankind has not shared in
our good fortune. On the one hand the industrial
revolution freed man from his slavery to the forces
of nature, but on the other it enslaved him to the
engines of production. Technology made possible a
more humane, healthier existence for all, but it
did not automatically extend its benefits to a
majority of the world's peoples. The communications revolution led to rising expectations followed by deep resentments, enormous hopes, and massive alienation. With the revolution in technology,
we have witnessed many times the steady rise and
fall of national leaders who were unable to deliver

the good life to their constituents, not simply because of personal limitations, but because of external forces beyond their control. Liberation from colonialism, accordingly, has not brought liberation from poverty and despair, as so many hoped it would.

Despite its appeal to the Christian conscience, liberation theology, like those types that have preceded it, is probably too culture-bound to satisfy contemporary needs for a set of principles that can provide guidance for a global policy on human rights. We have seen in these discussions how differently the cultures of nations with a common Christian heritage consider the issues of human rights and social order. Western Europe, the United States, Latin America, Russia, Ethiopia, and many other African nations look back to a common religious origin, and yet they balance their desires for social order and individual liberty quite differently. Increasingly, complexity is introduced by the consideration of the non-Christian cultures of Asia, Africa, and the Middle East, all of which express their interest in the rights and responsibilities of the individual in their own ways.

Nevertheless, we are not satisfied to leave the matter there. Two epochs, millennia apart in time, bespeak mankind's sense that a life of dignity and freedom is the birthright of every human being. The first, an "axial age" in human history, first explicated by Alfred Weber and popularized by Karl Jaspers, seems to have occurred in China, India, the Middle East, and the Mediterranean over a period of eleven centuries beginning in the ninth century B.C. All the normative philosophies that underlie our contemporary civilizations came into being in that era. Among the seminal religious seers and philosophers whose wisdom guides us to this day, only Mohammad, the last of the prophets,

234

came later, and his insights rest on those of his predecessors. Whatever our cultural heritage, therefore, we are guided by the principles of the great thinkers of that axial period in human history when, in the words of Jaspers, "Man as we know him today, came into being."

The other critical epoch is our own, the atomic age, when for the first time mankind is bound together by communications and technology; by common needs, hopes, and fears; where for the first time in history global interdependence has become a reality and global destruction a possibility.

Common to us all, therefore, is a pluralistic intellectual heritage of perceptive leaders by whom our civilizations came into being. Common to us all is the prospect of a future that demands rededication to that heritage. Today, as never before, the heritage of one can become the heritage of all. Therefore, we know that despite our present inability to find solutions to the problems of universal human rights, we must pursue that quest, searching for ways to fashion out of our cultural and historical diversity a world of equity and justice.

IMPLICATIONS FOR AMERICAN FOREIGN POLICY

KENNETH W. THOMPSON

The aim of this volume has been to explore the
underlying assumptions and premises of human rights
in different political cultures. It has traced
similarities and differences that result from different cultural traditions and political, philosophical, and theological systems. By implication it
has asked how universal is the concept of human
rights as understood in the United States and certain Western countries. What remains is a discussion of the implications of these findings for the
conduct of American foreign policy.

Much of the debate concerning the place of human
rights in United States foreign policy has come to
involve questions not of premises but of tactics.
Considering the importance of Saudi Arabia to the
American economy, is this the time to press for
equal rights for women? Considering our leverage
arising out of South Korean dependence on our military presence and support, ought we not press for
greater liberalization? Considering the delicacy
and complexity of current negotiations, isn't it
better to ignore the state of human rights in the
People's Republic of China? Considering our role
as donor nation, shouldn't we press in the developing countries, in the first instance, for the fulfillment of basic human needs? Considering the
fundamental importance of limiting strategic

237

nuclear arms, shouldn't we mute our criticism of
Soviet treatment of dissidents and would-be emigrés?

Behind all such questions, no matter how passion-
ately held the opposing answers, is the appearance
of a widely shared assumption that for the United
States it is a moral imperative to advance human
rights everywhere. This premise has gone largely
unexamined.

Put another way, the current wisdom is that the
advancement of human rights is a constant goal of
United States foreign policy in all settings.
Whether and how much we press toward that goal in a
specific instance depends upon the particular configurations of our other goals and of our power.
Considerations of national security or economic advantage or geographic location may render us
situationally impotent or inadequate. But the
rectitude of the goal remains, an ever-present
cause for rededication to its universal validity.

Some Americans who accept human rights as a universal moral imperative are sensitive to the charge
that it is really a parochial American political
imperative with little moral standing outside the
traditions of Western civilization. The convention-
al counter to that charge is to invoke the sanctity
of international and comparative law.

Starting with the Charter of the United Nations,
it is possible to point to a long list of multilateral declarations, covenants, treaties, agreements, and undertakings through which states--many,
if not all--have committed themselves, to greater
or lesser degree, to respect and advance either
human rights in general or particular ones. It is
also possible to point to a large number of constitutions and other fundamental laws promulgated
since 1945 (and earlier) in which governments of

particular nation-states have committed themselves, not always without ambiguity, to respect the fundamental freedoms of their citizenry and to advance economic and social justice, rights or goals. The importance of all this law making, it is said, is that it demonstrates that human rights, no matter how rooted in Western and American traditions, have become universal moral goods--desired by all persons in all nations of modern times. Thus, the argument concludes, in advancing human rights, the United States is not imposing a parochial morality on others but, rather, aligning itself with others' efforts to realize a morality common to all.

Many of the studies in this volume call into question the validity of these policy premises. Some do so by searching out the critical concepts through which the individual and the state have been linked in the traditions of non-Western political cultures. What becomes clear is that it is primarily in the political tradition of the West that individual rights vis-à-vis the state came to be asserted, exercised, declared inalienable, and enshrined in positive law as a central organizing principle of government itself.

Non-Western traditions are notably different and the differences are not simply semantic, with different cultures using different words and symbols to point to the same underlying reality. What is at issue are various understandings of the underlying reality itself. Cultures differ in the understandings they have of such fundamentals as the nature and destiny of man; the existence, nature, and role of the divine, of time, of truth, and of history. These fundamentals within each culture help shape characteristic concepts of the good life and of the individual, social, and political practices and arrangements appropriate to its pursuit or attainment.

In this perspective, not only the concept of "rights," but also the concept of "law" embodied in modern constitutionalism and international treaties, can be seen as typically Western, not universal. This suggests that democratic constitutions, whether liberal or socialist, promulgated in non-Western countries must be seen, not as harbingers of the global institutionalization of democracy and human rights, but as cultural aberrations too often overwhelmed by the resurgence of traditional political concepts and practices.

Similarly, developments in international law--including the U.N. Charter and the Universal Declaration of Human Rights--must be seen, not as bringing state power effectively under the rule of law, but as reaffirmations of what international law has always been: a device through which satisfied powers legitimate the power that supports their concepts of justice and seek to protect it against the revisionist demands of the dissatisfied. This quality of international law, plus its obvious Western origins, gives it standing with non-Western states only when that is convenient. Thus the most lasting universal feature of international law is the hypocrisy with which all states proclaim their support for it. It provides a weak reed on which to rest a claim for universal righteousness.

If human rights have neither the universal moral validity nor the global legal standing usually claimed for them, what are the implications for a United States policy on human rights that is premised on such claims? Or, to put the question differently, what place would human rights have in a U.S. foreign policy that assumes that human rights have neither universal moral validity nor global legal standing? It is a question to which at least two kinds of answers are possible.

One answer would be for United States policy to dedicate itself to converting the world to what the U.S. acknowledges to itself are Western, not universal, values. Such a policy would no doubt quickly see advantages to claiming universal standing for the values. The end result would be a policy whose main difference from present policy would be in its deliberate cynicism.

Another answer would be for United States policy to accept cultural diversity and moral disunity as conditions of international politics for the immediate future, and a worldwide search for new precepts of international morality. Such a policy would have many characteristics, and three central ones are discussed below.

First, the advancement of human rights would cease to be an all-controlling supreme objective in the conduct of current foreign policy. The treatment by a foreign government of its population would cease to be a matter for continuous official public comment in this country except in those cases in which it is judged that such comment would have a positive impact upon United States security or other tangible interests. Otherwise, in cases of particularly inhumane treatment, quiet diplomacy would be used to limit the most blatant forms of man's inhumanity to man. (Full implementation of such policy restraint would have to await congressional action that rescinded legislation requiring the Executive Branch to comment publicly upon human rights practices in certain groups of foreign countries.)

This would not, of course, stop other governments from hurling human rights charges at one another. The Soviet Union has become particularly fond of mounting human rights campaigns against governments it seeks to weaken. This means that

American officials will at times be drawn into using the language of human rights as an instrument of policy, if only to prevent others from monopolizing the concept for ideological purposes.

Which leads to a second point. United States officials should disassociate themselves from the fiction embodied in U.N. documents that there exist social and economic rights such as those advanced by Communist adversaries of equal standing with those civil and political rights that are the very essence of Western democracy. This fiction makes it impossible to clarify the difference between democracy on the one hand and authoritarian and totalitarian regimes on the other. With this fiction, leaders of oppressive regimes can claim that their citizens, however tyrannized, nonetheless enjoy "human rights" because social and economic benefits are justly distributed.

Just distribution of social and economic benefits is, of course, a paramount goal of democratic societies, but a goal to be pursued through the assurance of civil and political rights, not at their cost. The exercise of these rights may result in citizens being given, through legislation, certain "rights" or entitlements to social or economic benefits. The history of social and economic legislation demonstrates the American commitment to advancing the good society. But such rights are discretionary, subject to legislative change. They thus differ from the "fundamental civil and political rights that are constitutional and inalienable --absolutely essential to the democratic character of the political system. "Liberty and justice for all" is the democratic ideal, but liberty is the irreducible democratic reality.

This is not to say, of course, that all political systems must be or can be organized around this democratic principle. But it is a principle that Americans should be concerned to have properly understood by politically conscious people in all cultures, for two reasons. One is that such people will find it difficult to escape Communist rhetoric which uses the vocabulary of democracy and rights to carry a nondemocratic message. A second reason is that such people may find occasion to wish to experiment with democracy. To urge that American officials cease preaching that human rights are the key to universal political salvation is not to advise that the American democratic model be hidden under a bushel. There are people who love freedom in every culture and they are not served by America's depreciation of its central political tenets.

One clear way to discourage the bogus importance currently assigned to social and economic rights would be for the president to withdraw from the Senate his request of February 23, 1978, for its advice and consent to ratification of the International Covenant on Economic, Social and Cultural Rights, while allowing to stand his request pertaining to the International Covenant on Civil and Political Rights.

There is a third and more profound point to be made about the nature and content of a United States foreign policy that does not rest on the premise of the universal moral and legal validity of human rights. Contrary to what many would claim or fear, such a foreign policy need not be devoid of moral content. Policy would have moral content if its overriding purpose were not just to provide security for the nation but to make individual liberty secure in the nation. A secure police state would be a moral abomination. The moral bankruptcy of United States foreign policy will be at hand, if ever the choice before the nation is between guns and liberty. In brief, there is substantial moral content to a national policy that seeks national security in the international arena and "liberty and justice for all" at home.

Moreover, to question the universal moral validity of the concept of individual civil and political rights is not to say that people in all cultures do not have a great deal in common. It is to say, however, that mankind does not share a single, common vision of the good life; that no dominant philosophy of history, no single moral framework unites mankind. This is hardly a new condition. International society remains pluralist in character. But in an era of growing populations, armed with weapons of extinction, pressing the environment to its limits, and increasingly involved in one another's lives, it is a condition fraught with dangers to human survival. To press the search for a common vision would seem a matter of highest urgency and one to which the world's best minds should be summoned.

Is there anything United States foreign policy can do to help press the search? For one thing it could recognize that to expose the fraudulence of Soviet universality it is not necessary to proclaim that the American vision is adequate for all. If American leaders can muster that degree of modesty, then American cultural and educational exchange programs might begin to display a greater interest in mutuality and reciprocity. Thus, for example, foreign intellectual, cultural, and religious leaders could be brought to this country as teachers and fellow searchers, not just as foreign "influentials" to be exposed to American society. Americans might also dust off their interest in the United Nations University and ask what its plans and programs could contribute to the search for a common vision.

What these examples suggest is that the direct
contribution of United States foreign policy to
the search for a common vision will be long range,
endless, and unspectacular. It is also likely to
be unavailing unless the American people can combine an abiding faith in their own political
vision with a willingness to listen to and learn
from others. Simultaneously, others will learn
more from the American political system the more
it succeeds in delivering "liberty and justice for
all." For the immediate future such a course may
be the best measure of the moral quality of United
States foreign policy. It involves dignity in pursuing worthy and noble ends both in the national
and the world's interest, but not for reasons of
domestic politics or "to make Americans feel good."
It demands being on guard against the American
tendency toward national self-righteousness, of
which Alexis de Tocqueville wrote: "It is impossible
to conceive a more troublesome and garrulous
patriotism." It requires the moral courage to
speak out when true crises require it and to practice self-restraint in time of pseudo-crises and to
distinguish between real alarms and false ones. It
calls for political wisdom to be firm in the truth
but to resist fruitless international contentious-
ness. It necessitates rediscovering and practicing
the enduring and unique truths enshrined in the
American political tradition without ceaselessly
proclaiming or forcibly imposing our virtues on
others. It means turning to others, not in weakness but in strength, to help shape the answers to
moral and political problems. In the simplest, most
basic terms and despite popular expectations and
public clamor, it entails thinking before we speak,
planning before we promote, and being wise before
we are clever. We need new formulations of
ancient truths and patient men whose perceptions we
can trust. The world needs an updated public
philosophy from America that conserves what is true

and combines it with what men of good will everywhere are seeking. Presidential speechwriters and
strategists are not providing a framework or
philosophy.

If this diagnosis of the American foreign policy
problem is sound, voluntary groups such as the
Council on Religion and International Affairs have
a mandate and an urgent mission. To search for
moral and political truths, to see them in their
interrelations and not in isolation, to order and
balance them and not merely enunciate them ought to
be someone's business. CRIA's aim, however modest-
ly pursued, is to initiate public discussion of
moral and political issues without claiming the
skills of those who must implement public policy.
Mobilizing concern for these issues will be the
ongoing task of CRIA, following Socrates, who wrote:
"the unexamined life is not worth living."

STUDY GROUP ON HUMAN RIGHTS AND FOREIGN POLICY
Council on Religion and International Affairs

Co-Chairmen

William L. Bradley
President
The Hazen Foundation

E. Raymond Platig
Director
Office of External Research
Department of State

****

William J. Barnds
Senior Research Fellow
Council on Foreign
  Relations
Chairman of the Board,
  CRIA

Adda B. Bozeman
Professor Emeritus of
  International Affairs
Sarah Lawrence College

E. Ralph Buultjens
Professor of Interna-
tional Politics
New School for Social
  Research

James F. Childress
Kennedy Center for
  Bioethics
Georgetown University

David Dell
Consultant, Educational
  Programs, CRIA

James Finn
Editor, *Worldview*
Director of Publica-
  tions, CRIA

Alan Geyer
Executive Director
Center for Theology
  and Public Policy

Norman Graebner
Professor of History
University of Virginia

J. Bryan Hehir
Associate Secretary
Office of International
  Justice and Peace
U.S. Catholic Conference

Charles P. Henderson
Senior Minister
Central Presbyterian Church
New York City

John Herz
Professor, City College,
  retired

Alistair Jessiman
Research Associate
Carnegie Center for
  Transnational Studies
Student, Dartmouth College

247

Philip A. Johnson
President, CRIA

Edward L. Keenan
Professor of History
Dean, Graduate School of
    Arts and Sciences
Harvard University

Asmarom Legesse
Department of Anthropology
Swarthmore College

S.C. Leng
Doherty Professor of
    Government
Chairman, Asian Studies
    Committee
University of Virginia

Sidney Liskofsky
Director, Division of
    International Organiza-
    tions
American Jewish Committee

Gilburt D. Loescher
Assistant Professor
Department of Government
    and International
    Studies
University of Notre Dame
Fellow, Institute for the
    Study of World Politics

Jeffrey Merritt
Fellow
Institute for the Study
    of World Politics

Hans J. Morgenthau
University Professor
New School for Social
    Research

Stephen Paschke
Associate Director
Institute for the Study
    of World Politics

Roger Shinn
Union Theological
    Seminary, New York

Donald W. Shriver, Jr.
President
Union Theological
    Seminary, New York

Kenneth W. Thompson
Commonwealth Professor of
    Government and Foreign
    Affairs
University of Virginia
Director, Studies in
    Ethics and Foreign
    Policy, CRIA

Sandra Vogelgesang
International Affairs
    Fellow
Council on Foreign
    Relations

Malcolm Warford
Director of Educational
    Research
Associate Professor of
    Religion and Education
Union Theological
    Seminary, New York

Coordinator
Ulrike Klopfer
Assistant to the
    President, CRIA

248